FROM TROUBLE to TRIUMPH

TRUE STORIES OF REDEMPTION FROM DRUGS, GANGS & PRISON

Alisha M. Rosas

Introduction by
Luis J. Rodriguez

Tía Chucha Press
Los Angeles

ISBN 978-1-882688-54-8

Book design: Jane Brunette
Cover art: Freddy "Coyote" Negrete

Published by:

Tia Chucha Press
A Project of Tia Chucha's Centro Cultural, Inc.
PO Box 328
San Fernando, CA 91341
www.tiachucha.com

Distributed by:

Northwestern University Press
Chicago Distribution Center
11030 South Langley Avenue
Chicago, IL 606028

Tía Chucha's Centro Cultural & Bookstore is a 501 (c) (3) nonprofit corporation funded in part over the years by the National Endowment for the Arts, California Arts Council, Los Angeles County Arts Commission, Los Angeles Department of Cultural Affairs, The California Community Foundation, the Annenberg Foundation, the Weingart Foundation, the Lia Fund, National Association of Latino Arts and Culture, Ford Foundation, MetLife, Southwest Airlines, the Andy Warhol Foundation for the Visual Arts, the Thrill Hill Foundation, the Middleton Foundation, Center for Cultural Innovation, John Irvine Foundation, Not Just Us Foundation, the Attias Family Foundation, and the Guacamole Fund, among others. Donations have also come from Bruce Springsteen, John Densmore of The Doors, Jackson Browne, Lou Adler, Richard Foos, Gary Stewart, Charles Wright, Adrienne Rich, Tom Hayden, Dave Marsh, Jack Kornfield, Jesus Trevino, David Sandoval, Gary Soto, Denise Chávez and John Randall of the Border Book Festival, Luis & Trini Rodríguez, and others.

Contents

Homegirls, 1972.

PREFACE
No Greater Honor

AS A LITTLE GIRL, I used to watch my (now late) grandmother, Rosie Rosas, with people. They always talked with her openly, sharing their stories, even though she was a stranger to them. She would joke she carried the letter "P" on her forehead—branding her as a "psychologist" when she gave advice, or for pendeja when listening to one of their stories made her late to an errand.

I always knew it was much more than that. My grandmother had a way about her that connected her to others. I would watch her listen to a young mother in a grocery store line, or an old man at the doctor's office, and it seemed that in their exchanged laughter or concerned looks, a sense of family formed, if only for a few moments.

If writing this book taught me anything, it is that my grandmother is very much alive in me. As I sat and listened to the life stories of these men—Narciso, Antonio, Jess, Mike, Freddy, and Jesse—I was humbled by how much they were willing to share with me. A kinship formed between each of them and myself. Earning their trust and hearing their words was a privilege. But getting the opportunity to retell their stories here, well, there is no greater honor.

I hope their stories awaken a sense of hope in you, dear reader, of how not all labels last forever and how sometimes it really is as English theologian and historian Thomas Fuller described, "darkest just before the dawn." Stories of redemption are among us wherever struggle has lived. I hope these stories touch your heart as much as they have my own.

—*Alisha M. Rosas*

LUIS OUTSIDE OF SOLEDAD PRISON AFTER HIS TALK THERE, 2010.

INTRODUCTION

Owning One's Life: A New Narrative on Gangs, Prisons, and Addictions

Luis J. Rodriguez

THERE'S A MAJOR NARRATIVE in the United States about gang members, prisoners, and drug addicts: *they can never change.* "Once a gang member, always a gang member," is one refrain. In this age of mass incarceration, poor people, mostly black and brown, but also whites, Native Americans, and Asians, have been given decades behind bars, warehoused and largely forgotten. All girded by this narrative, which has driven policies and maddening laws like "three strikes and you're out," trying youth as adults, gang and gun enhancements, gang injunctions, and more. The U.S. now houses 25 percent of the world's prison population, although we are only 5 percent of the world's population.

California leads the way. In the early 1970s, the state had 15 prisons with 15,000 people. Today it has 34 facilities with upwards of 170,000. It's the second largest prison system in the world after the U.S. federal system. The largest ethnic group is Chicano/Latino; the most disproportionate is African American. Around 70 percent are black and brown. I call the California Department of Corrections the largest publically funded poor people's housing in the state.

To challenge that narrative, I offer the stories in this book of veteran members from two Los Angeles-area gangs— *Lomas* and *Sangra*. Their *placasos* (gang monikers) are Chuco, Tonito, Lil'Yuk, Chino, Coyote, and Chuy. They are also fathers, grandfathers, husbands, and now sober and positive contributors to their community. Their family names are Narciso Espinoza, Antonio Fierro, Jess Montecino, Mike Moreno, Freddy Negrete, and Jesse Olivas. They were once hard-core *cholo* gang members, drugs addicts, and prisoners. They are also my homies and friends.

I WAS PART OF THE LOMAS STREET GANG in the late 1960s and early 1970s. This was a mostly Chicano (Mexicans born or raised in the U.S.) barrio considered one of the poorest neighborhoods in Los Angeles County at the time. Our main rival was from a smaller but tough barrio surrounding the old San Gabriel Mission called Sangra. San Gabriel was L.A.'s first settlement when the Spanish arrived, although Native peoples like the Tongva, Tataviam, and Chumash had thriving villages on this land for tens of thousands of years before any missions were built. Mexican migrants settled in the San Gabriel area in significant numbers during the 1930s and 1940s.

In the 1970s, a national magazine called the war between Lomas and Sangra one of the bloodiest in the country. By age 18,

LOMAS MURAL.

I lost 25 friends from both neighborhoods to gang violence, heroin overdoses, police killings, suicides, and similar calamities.

Lomas was located in the Garvey Hills in an unincorporated community called South San Gabriel. Las Lomas in Spanish means "The Hills." For some time, local gang youth chanted, "The Hills Kills for Thrills." Poetry and art never stops, even in the ghettos (home of Hip Hop and more), barrios (lowriding, black & gray tattoos, *cholo* style clothing), reservations, or trailer parks of the country. Even if informed with death, fatalism, trauma.

A little history: during the late 1800s, Natives and Mexicans (which included many Natives from Mexico) ended up in the Garvey Hills after being hounded following the invasion of the United States that led to the U.S.-Mexico war. That war ended in 1848. Native Americans were particularly hunted down with mutilations and killings when bounties were placed on their heads (and bonds voted on to raise the funds) following the 1849 gold rush. With Spanish conquistadors and their disastrous rule; oppressive and exploitative Mexican governance; and then the United States invasion, the Native American population went from an estimated one million people in the 1500s to 16,000 by 1900. More than a 90 percent drop in the Native population from 1850 to 1900. There's a street in the Garvey Hills called "Graves" that a chronicler of the area told me was named for the Natives and Mexicans buried there.

In the 1930s, white migrants called "Okies" and "Arkies" populated South San Gabriel after they were forced to leave the "Dust Bowl." They established a baseball park, "Rebel Field," in deference to their Southern roots. The "Wilmar Donkeys" street association was supposedly named after Wilmar, Arkansas. Yet another more plausible account was that the name came from combining the first letters of two areas, Willetts (named for a settler) and Del Mar (Spanish for "of the ocean") to become "Wilmar." Either way some of the youth had a tattoo of "Wilmar" above a donkey's head.

By the 1940s, most migrant communities in the vast San Gabriel Valley (SGV) became Mexican, including South San Gabriel. These migrants picked fruit and nuts, mostly citrus and walnuts. The SGV barrios had names like Monte Flores (Mountain Flowers from a nursery), Canta Ranas (Singing Frogs), El Jardin (The Garden), La Puente (the bridge), Cherryville (in Pomona for the cherry pickers), and migrant settlements such as El Monte's Hicks and Hayes camps. Around a hundred other barrios were also established in this valley, many in unincorporated areas.

1940s PACHUCA.

BARRIO HOME.

At the same time, especially during and after World War II when SGV became industrialized, Mexican railroad and factory workers nestled next to the San Gabriel Mission, a few miles north of South San Gabriel. The Sangra neighborhood had small homes, cramped apartments, dirt alleys. The Wham-O Toy Company, makers of Frisbees and Hula-Hoops, had a manufacturing plant in San Gabriel.

In my teens, Las Lomas had no sidewalks, abandoned cars in ravines, shacks for homes, goats and chickens in backyards. Both Lomas and Sangra were surrounded by some of the first U.S. suburbs, built mostly for white professional or skilled workers on top of former farmlands.

By the 1960s, South San Gabriel was bounded by the incorporated cities of Montebello to the south; Rosemead to the north; Monterey Park to the west; and the parkland Whittier Narrows to the east. These relatively well-off suburbs had sidewalks, paved roads, and shopping malls. In some places, Mexicans were not allowed.

I remember as a child walking through a small park in one of these suburbs and being chased out by white residents. Decades later, after an influx of mostly Mexican and Asian residents, I threw the first baseball for a multi-ethnic Little League at the same park.

The SGV is now home to the largest Asian populations in the U.S.—from Japan, Taiwan, Hong Kong, Korea, Vietnam, and Mainland China. White flight in the 1980s opened up housing. Many Chicano barrios were "gentrified," including most of Las Lomas (streets are now paved and there are mansions and town houses next to the remaining barrio homes). Upwardly mobile Chicanos moved into these formerly white suburbs next to Asian transplants. Poorer Chicanos just kept moving east, toward the deserts.

Despite being largely pushed out, the Lomas gang grew—spreading out to Rosemead, West Covina, and other parts of the Valley. One of the first gang injunctions ever instituted was in the early 1980s, in West Covina, targeting Lomas and other eastward-moving barrio gangs. Gang injunctions are where police can implement strict curfews, break up two or more persons on corners, interrogate any tattooed person or someone holding

BARRIO STREET SCENE.

a bat, put suspected gang members on a statewide database (nearly impossible to be removed from), and more.

Los Angeles currently has 40 gang injunctions, suppressing some 70 neighborhoods, all communities of color. Yet, like elsewhere, gang warfare intensified in the SGV, prompting one Chicano Rap group of the 1990s, The D.O.P.E. Mob, to call this "The Valley of Death."

MY OWN STORY THERE begins in a poor section of Monterey Park where my family moved from Watts (with a brief foray into the San Fernando Valley) when I was eight years old. Eleven of us lived in a two-bedroom apartment with my oldest sister, her husband, their two daughters, my mom, dad, us four kids—and a grandmother or aunt from time to time. Most of the kids slept on blankets in the living room. Tensions ran high. After one family member stabbed another, everyone was evicted.

With the help of a poverty agency, my dad found a one-bedroom wood frame home in the flatlands of South San Gabriel (once part of "Wilmar," the City of Rosemead later annexed it). My dad, mom, and two sisters slept in the living room. My brother and I were stuck in a tiny bedroom. The street had no sidewalks and dead-ended at a cornfield, where neighborhood kids often played. I recall the white owner chasing us with a shotgun and firing bird pellets (the cornfield is now gone, home to Edison Company's offices).

At the time, South San Gabriel had many unpaved streets. Youth here established a car club of poor whites and Mexicans called Chug-A-Lug. By the late 1960s, other street clubs included Thee Animal Tribe, which incorporated many of the South San Gabriel and Rosemead barrio youth. However, Las Lomas during this time began heavy recruitment and these clubs (including the Southside Boys, Little Gents, Thee Ravens, Thee Mystics, and Thee Illusions) eventually became part of Lomas cliques. These consisted of *Pequeños* (Pee Wees, ages six to 12); *Dukes* (ages 12-14); *Chicos* (ages 14-18); *Locos* (the hard core gang youth, mostly 15 and above); and *Veteranos* (the older

LUIS AS A TEEN.

homies, many of whom gained their status in prison). San Gabriel also had street clubs like Thee Escorts, Regents, and Chancellors. Those got incorporated into Sangra *klikas*, including their most well known, *Diablos*.

Other street associations that emerged out of South San Gabriel and surrounding communities include The Groupe (one of the oldest and largest lowrider car clubs) as well as the Mongols motorcycle club, a mostly Mexican-and-white "1 percenter" organization. The Mongols once went to war with the Hell's Angels. Law enforcement has labeled them one of the most violent biker gangs in the country.

When I was 13, my dad bought a two-bedroom home in the southern part of the City of San Gabriel for $12,500, one of the few Mexican families to own homes there. Also tied to "Wilmar," San Gabriel had already annexed this area. I helped recruit local youth into Lomas to keep this area away from Sangra. Over the years this led to the formation of the *Norwood Locos* clique of Las Lomas.

In my youth, I had arrests for rioting (Chicano Moratorium

Chicano Moratorium against the vietnam war.

Against the Vietnam War), and being placed in Murderer's Row of the old Hall of Justice Jail for possible murder charges, as well as stealing, fighting, disturbing the peace, and attempted murder. I spent nights in East L.A. and San Gabriel Valley jails, in juvenile hall, and two adult facilities. Despite this, I never received convictions until 18 years of age.

I'd been using heavy drugs, including heroin, since age 12. I'd been shot at half-a-dozen times, including machine gun fire and at point-blank range, yet never hit. I got kicked out of three high schools and thrown out of my house at 15 (and briefly homeless), before moving into a small room in my family's garage with no running water and no heat. Fortunately, community activists mentored me out of this life—so that I later returned to high school and obtained my diploma. I become part of the radical wing of the Chicano Movement for Civil Rights. I also painted eight murals, tried to play saxophone, as well as partake in Mexica (Aztec) dance, amateur boxing, martial arts, photography, and community organizing.

I continued to be active in Lomas until 19. A year before, I avoided a state prison term for intervening on behalf of a hand-cuffed young Chicana as sheriff's deputies beat her while she lay on the ground (a decidedly non-gangster act, a marked change in my role as barrio warrior). I faced a minimum of six years. Community members wrote letters on my behalf, convincing a judge to give me a break (not a second chance—more like a fifth or sixth chance). My convictions for resisting arrest and disturbing the peace led to time served in the L.A. County Men's Jail. I began my first heroin withdrawals there, and after my release I vowed never to go back.

Holding my newborn son, Ramiro, when I was 20, transformed my life. Although I had 20 more years of drinking and rage issues to deal with (and later Ramiro joined a Chicago street gang and ended up serving almost 15 years in prison), I never returned to *the crazy life*. Now Ramiro and I are reconciled. He's been released from prison for close to seven years—gang-free, drug-free, and crime-free. My daughter Andrea and other sons, Ruben and Luis, are grown up. I also have five grandchildren and three great-grandchildren.

I've been blessed beyond measure. However, I never forgot those left behind. I began peace efforts in the 1970s with the End Barrio Warfare Coalition, Centro Del Pueblo, and others. In 1980, I did my first prison workshops in writing and healing at Chino prison. Since then I've visited San Quentin, Soledad, Folsom, and Lancaster prisons (where I've been doing creative writing workshops at various times across ten years), as well as countless juvenile lockups and camps. I also worked in prisons across the United

Section of mural by Luis J. Rodriguez, 1971.

States, particularly in Illinois, and in countries like Mexico, El Salvador, Guatemala, Argentina, Italy, and England.

CHUCO AND CHUY are contemporary homeboys of mine. Lil' Yuk, Tonito, and Chino are from younger generations. Coyote is another contemporary from Sangra. Coyote—Freddy—and I know of at least one occasion when we've shot at each other. Freddy and I are now *camaradas*. Today I don't consider any barrio my enemy, or hold any grudges, regardless of the ongoing warfare that still haunts these streets. I've been for urban peace, social justice, and economic equity for close to 45 years.

We were all among that generation first impacted by the massive influx of war weapons and drugs during and following the Vietnam War, an influx that escalated by the 1980s. These men are the *vatos* who survived—we lost so many homies during that time, and many more in subsequent years. At the same time, this kind of warfare spread out exponentially over the past 50 years so that today at least a million young people are involved in street gangs at some level in this country. The majority are black and brown, but the greatest rise is among whites, Native Americans, Asians. Thousands more are now across Mexico, Central America, the Caribbean, and other countries due to deportations as well as mass culture (Gangsta Rap, movies, etc.). Gunfire has become the soundtrack of our times.

While a few of the guys in this book came from hardworking, law-abiding families (me included), others did not (one homie's parents were heroin addicts). What united us were systemic poverty and discrimination as well as a growing trade in guns and drugs that began in the 1970s and went hog wild crazy during the 1980s and 1990s—the worse period of gang violence in U.S. history.

We somehow got caught in the web of barrio experiences that began from 1910-1940 with Mexican *pachuco* (zootsuited) youth. They were the sons and daughters of refugees from the Mexican Revolution and other upheavals (1910-1929), which claimed a million lives, and resulted in close to a million

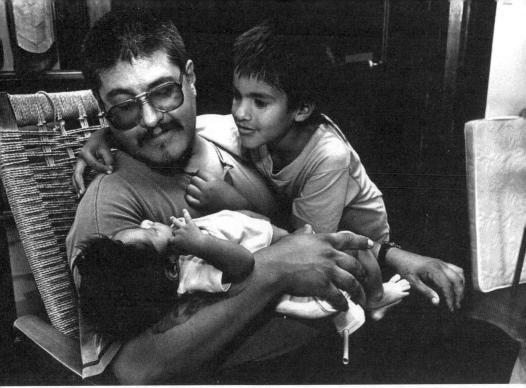

LUIS WITH HIS YOUNGEST SONS RUBEN AND CHITO, 1994, CHICAGO.

refugees, when Mexico had 15 million people, about the size of Guatemala today.

The mass media represented these *pachucos* as unrepentant delinquents before and after the so-called 1943 "Zootsuit Riots," when sailors, police, and other whites attacked Mexicans, but also blacks and Filipinos. Extra policing, mostly with racist whites, including former "Okies" and "Arkies," targeted these youth leading to mass arrests. By the late 1950s, Chicano gangs from the Los Angeles area were dominating the major state prisons. They successfully confronted whites and blacks for power in the prison system and the streets. Their only real challenge came from other Chicanos in northern and central California migrant barrios. Since the early 1970s, this conflict has been called the *Norteño* and *Sureño* wars ("Northern" and "Southern" in Spanish), which has led to countless deaths across the state.

Cholos, which inherited the *pachuco* traditions, emerged in the 1950s and led to greater barrio gang consolidation. Today

ACTIVIST LEADERS IN CHICANO HIGH SCHOOL STUDENT ORGANIZATION, 1972

in Los Angeles city alone there are more than 500 Chicano/ Latino street gangs with around 200 African American gangs. For the past four decades, Los Angeles and Chicago have contended for "gang capital" of the country, both also being the largest manufacturing centers (having lost thousands of jobs during the deindustrialization and outsourcing that began in the mid-1970s).

In addition, the biggest rise in gangs nationally was largely due to Los Angeles and Chicago gangs, primarily after poor communities got squeezed out. Throughout the U.S., you'll find L.A.-based *Sureño 13* gangs (like 18th Street, Florencia, White Fence, Mara Salvatrucha, and others) and Bloods & Crips—as well as Folk & People gangs from Chicago (Latin Kings, Gangster Disciples, Vice Lords, Spanish Cobras, and many more). For example, a few Lomas gang members apparently ended up in Omaha, Nebraska, during the 1990s, creating the second largest gang there (although Omaha has hardly any "hills" like in L.A.).

Since the 1992 Los Angeles Uprising, following the acquittal of police officers involved in the Rodney King beating (becoming the worst civil disturbance in the U.S. since the 1960s), the federal government went after undocumented youth for deportations. These increased after a 1996 immigration bill aimed at non-status persons who had spent time in jail. A million migrants or so have been deported under these conditions, the vast majority to Mexico and Central America, including former children of refugees from civil wars in El Salvador, Guatemala, Nicaragua, and Honduras of the 1970s and 1980s.

Unfortunately, a critical number were in L.A.-based gangs, enough to change cultures.

There have now been around 25 years of *cholo* type gang cultures in El Salvador, Guatemala, and Honduras (as well as parts of Mexico), contributing to the most homicidal areas in the world. My understanding is there are *cholo*-like tattooed deported youth in Cambodia and Armenia. In Japan, Taiwan, Thailand, Brazil, and Spain, lowriding and *cholo*-styles are important subcultures.

OF COURSE, THIS IS ONLY ONE SIDE OF THE STORY. Here, in your hands, is the other side—how some of these troubled men, with decades in La Vida Loca, have turned their life around—and have also sacrificed to help others. Men like Narciso, Antonio, Jess, Mike, Freddy, and Jesse.

I've met similar peace warriors elsewhere. I worked on peace plans in Chicago, where I lived for 15 years, including with the Increase the Peace Network and Youth Struggling for Survival. I did similar work in the Lakota, Tohono O'odham, and Navajo reservations. From 2006-2008, I assisted 40 urban peace leaders, gang interventionists, and researchers in Los Angeles on a "Community-based Gang Intervention Model"—the most comprehensive of its kind—with the help of then City Councilman Tony Cardenas, now U.S. Congressman (this plan was also introduced as a congressional bill).

In 2010, I presented this model in England and brought it that same year to Ciudad Juarez, Mexico when it was the murder capital of the world. I've also used this model in El Salvador and Argentina. Twice in the 2000s, I went to Guatemala to deal with gang youth. In El Salvador, I conducted interviews with gang youth and their families in 1993, and helped broker a gang peace in 1996 with MS-13 and 18th Street in San Salvador (sabotaged by the Salvadoran government of the time).

LOMAS HOMIES, 1972.

In 2012 and 2013, I returned as part of a team of peace leaders to support a broader gang peace effort, again undermined by U.S. government interests as well as Salvadoran officials. In 2016, My wife Trini and I spent a month in Honduras teaching poetry to abandoned girls from violence and poverty (also at a coed bilingual school in San Pedro Sula).

Gang violence is solvable, but only when resources are aligned to needs, when the roots of poverty and inequality are fully dealt with, and punishment is replaced with rehabilitation, education, treatment, and a new societal basis for healthy lives. However, for the most part, political will is missing. Most responses are "band aids" or entirely off track. That old narrative about "no change," and billion-dollar industries in prisons and law enforcement, have been the biggest obstacles to adequately address gang violence.

I CAN GO ON AND ON. But it's time for you to hear from the peace warriors in this book. I thank writer and friend Alisha M. Rosas for working on these stories, in-between her own full-time work, marriage, and children. A special thanks to Jesse Olivas, who you'll see is a common link to many of these men's healing, and who also helped pull them together for the book.

Jesse and I are both sober for the same number of years, 24 as of 2017. And I thank the vatos herein for opening up their hearts.

While women's stories are missing, they are threaded throughout in these men's relationships with wives, daughters, girlfriends, sisters, and mothers. This book is about the work we have to do as men to live healthy and respectful lives, including tapping into emotional and soul depths so women stop carrying all the burden of raising our children and holding up community with little or no means (and with either absent or unhealthy, too often violent, men). It means recognizing everyone's particular genius and internal design—and to create solid foundations, inside any person and in the world—for these to bloom as fully as possible.

In the end, these men learned to own their lives, becoming walking miracles, not just walking wounded, and taking personal as well as social responsibility, either through intense and meaningful spiritual practices, family, work, and/or art. They're also giving back to the communities that have been set back with bad decision-making, racist and social class barriers, and dead-end policies. These men overcame the most dispiriting realities that prisons, as well as the "prisons" of drugs and rage, did to minimize their humanity and dignity. They did so with their own strong spirits aided by good choices, families, causes, and faith in God. I hope their stories fire up your hearts, your imaginations, for how things should be in this country and elsewhere. It's time we stopped the madness once and for all.

CHUCO

Narciso "Chuco" Espinoza

"YOU ARE GOING TO DIE EARLY, *CARNAL*," the older homeboy told him. "You're gonna die for this neighborhood before you turn 33-years-old."

The homeboy's prophecy had a lifetime impact on Narciso "Chuco" Espinoza. Not only did he believe the words, he embraced them. "It was a belief system that was given to me and I accepted it with all my heart. That was my fate. No one could change it."

Chuco was born in East Los Angeles and was the oldest of seven children to his mother, Barbara, and father, Narciso Sr. East L.A. was home, and Chuco vividly remembers the sense of community around him, with neighbors sharing tacos and tamales with each other. "We were like a big family," he recalled.

When he turned 9, his father moved him and his siblings into a house in South San Gabriel, but everything looked and felt different.

"The scenery was like a ranch," Chuco said. "Everything felt so spread apart. Dirt roads, no sidewalks, and a shack of a house my dad bought us."

Narciso Sr. and Barbara were hard workers. Chuco's father would spend his days working in factories, making carpet. In his spare time he fixed old cars. Barbara cooked and cleaned and watched the kids, who were often left to their own devices, which proved troublesome for Chuco.

By 13, he was smoking weed and drinking.

"My parents were so busy just trying to get by, they didn't see what was happening," Chuco said. "The stress of raising a family and making ends meet was affecting the entire neighborhood and parents were arguing and we would talk as homies about it and relate to each other.

"It was like the problems between our parents brought us as homies closer together."

Despite this, he warned his siblings to stay away from gang activity. "I didn't want them to be like me," he said. "Looking back, with my dad working all the time to support us, it felt like he was never there. I started to believe I was boss of the house. My dad would work to support us, but in his absence I decided I was in charge."

Shortly before his 14th birthday, Chuco was jumped into the Lomas barrio street gang. Six Lomas members beat him so he could earn his place. He was bloodied, but afterward they shook his hand to welcome him. When he went home, he tried to hide his injuries from his parents, but his sister saw him and immediately called for their dad.

Chuco still remembers the way his father looked at him.

"To this day, it hurts. Our eyes met and he saw a lost kid. He didn't even say anything. He knew he had lost control of me. He just looked me up and down and walked away. It was like he knew he couldn't do anything to save me, I was already too far gone."

Chuco is clear that his parents had nothing to do with the choices he made during his early teenage years. "I never saw my dad hit my mom and they rarely argued. I had a good childhood."

However, his father stopped talking to Chuco after that night and his mom only cried to acknowledge her son's gang activity.

"She never asked me about it, she just had sad eyes," he said. "I felt like no one was saying anything about me, so I decided I had to take care of my siblings even more so they wouldn't be like me.

"I mean, my parents took care of us, they provided and there was always food on the table, but they never told us they loved us or what we should do with ourselves. My dad was a prideful man from Mexico. He didn't show his emotions. And my mom never was affectionate with us.

Her mom had 12 kids and my grandfather was a truck driver, so I think that's all she knew: take care of the kids with what they need when your husband isn't there. She didn't know any other way."

Chuco started using drugs, preferring barbiturates. To support his habit he also started selling.

"By seventh grade, I was pretty well known," he remembered. "I was a pretty good student too. In fact I was elected treasurer of the student government."

He was always popular. He dressed to the nines with shoes he shined every morning and nicely pressed pants. "That's how I got the nickname 'Chuco.' I dressed like a *pachuco*. I learned how by looking at pictures of them in magazines and old family pictures."

Being treasurer meant Chuco had the key to the jukebox to manage the money it brought in from students. "We used to steal the money from it and buy alcohol or drugs with it."

One night, 14-year-old Chuco came home drunk and loaded. He did not know it, but his father was waiting for him inside the house. Narciso Sr., tired of his son's behavior, decided to do

something about it.

"He was right there at the door when I came in," Chuco remembered. "Just standing at the door. I felt so angry. What right did he have over me? All he did was work, but I was the one raising the family. I was in charge and now he wanted it back?"

His father lunged at him.

"Once he put his hands on me, I snapped," Chuco said. "That was the first time I swung and hit my father."

The memory still brings tears to his eyes. "I kept hitting him, but he was bigger, stronger, and he beat me to a pulp. He was taking all his anger out on me.

"Afterward, he took off all my clothes and took me to the bathroom. He plugged the tub and started to fill it with water. I knew what was coming. He was so angry with me for being the way I was that for a moment, I actually thought he was going to kill me."

Narciso Sr. threw Chuco in the water, face first, and stepped on his back to hold him down, drowning him. "He was showing me that he was the boss of the house, not me," Chuco said. "He let me up and threw me in my room, then threw a towel at me.

"Everyone had been asleep, but woke up with the commotion. I remember my siblings looking at me. He had made his point to them, too. I wasn't the boss anymore. I wasn't in charge of them or anything."

The next morning, I was angrier with my family than ever before. I felt once my dad took the power from me, I had no reason to be there. I decided to get more involved with Lomas, because at least there, I felt important."

He started getting close with Jesse "Chuy" Olivas, who was older and a leader of Lomas. It was Chuy who introduced him to heroin. He had his first fix at 15.

"That day launched my love for heroin. That love resulted in more than 30 years of struggling from its addiction," Chuco said. "It made me feel things I never felt before. I felt on top of the world. Of course, that feeling made me want to get into more trouble so I started robbing people and stealing more."

At this time, he only had As and Bs on his report card. Once, the principal called him to his office to tell him he had one of the highest IQs in the school. He was even offered a scholarship to Don Bosco High School, but the idea of an all-boys school did not interest him. He turned down the scholarship and decided to join the homeboys at Mark Keppel High School.

There were more fights, more stealing, more time in juvenile hall. By 17, he was living in his parents' garage, not completely kicked out of his parents' house, but not really welcomed, either.

One evening, to get beer for a party, Chuco and his homeboy went to rob a small liquor store. Chuco took his rifle and the friend took a truck.

"I remember the people being so scared in that store and me yelling and pointing my rifle at them," he recalled. "They all had their hands up so I decided to lock them all in the freezer so we could get away. We loaded the truck and left them inside that freezer."

Once at the party, Chuco and his friend showed the other homies all they had brought, but within minutes cops surrounded the place.

"They found the stolen stuff, they found the rifle, and they arrested all of us," he said. "So we are all inside the county jail and they start sending me notes telling me to take the heat, to take the blame for the whole thing. Chuy had just been released from prison and was on parole, so he did not want to go back.

The others had similar situations. They knew I was young and had no real record yet, so they wanted me to take the blame.

"At first I was like, 'Hell no, I'm not taking the heat for everyone,' but they were so pissed at me that I took the blame for all the charges, including robbery, two kidnapping charges, and two attempted murders for locking those people in that freezer. I got four years."

He was intimidated when he arrived at the youth correctional center in Norwalk. On his second day, he was asked by Lomas members inside to stab another inmate with a fork.

"I didn't want to do it, I mean, I didn't even know the guy, but they were testing me and I had to pass their tests. I was so scared doing it, but when it was over, I was placed on lockdown and given new charges, but it didn't matter because I knew I was accepted again, and that was the start of my prison gang activity."

Chuco continued his addiction and paid for it by committing crimes. He was in and out of jail and prison regularly. During his mid-20s, he started reflecting a bit on his life and wondered why he kept making the same mistakes in his life. His addiction never let him think clearly. He started looking for ways to get sent back to prison, where things were familiar and drugs were everywhere. He would walk the streets late at night in South San Gabriel and wait for a cop to pick him up for using. Back then, cops would simply check someone's arms for heroin track marks. If the marks were there that was an easy three- or six-month sentence.

"It was easier to be in prison or jail," he remembered. "It was like I was tired of robbing and tired of living my life the way I was and always doing things to be sent to prison. At least if I was already there, I was with my homies and we could get loaded together. I didn't have to do anything to get there if I was already there."

And once inside, his addiction ruled all. To feed it, he would do anything, including using old needles from the bottom of the trash bin in the prison infirmary.

CHUCO WITH HIS BROTHER, LITTLE CHUCO, AND VINTAGE CARS.

"I would take them and rinse them out. You're gambling with your life, but it's like it doesn't matter. Everything is Russian roulette, but I was supposed to die young, remember? Why did I care?"

He feared death and the older homeboy's prophecy, but he didn't think he could change it. It wasn't until he was 33 and in prison, and very much alive, that he started to rethink his life again.

BY 33 HE HAD FOUR CHILDREN, but had no relationship with any of them. His lifestyle didn't provide him any reason to think about being a father. He kept using, but found it did nothing for him anymore. The excitement was no longer there. Women weren't interesting to him anymore. Everything he cared about before didn't seem to matter and he knew it was time to seek help.

He decided one day to go to church with his sister. He had grown up going to church with his family and had once appreciated those values and he could see himself caring again. During the service, Chuco felt a bit uncomfortable, almost like he didn't belong there. At the end of the service the pastor asked if anyone needed prayer.

Chuco wanted to stand and ask for help, but his pride kept him silent. The pastor asked again.

"I felt this tug to get up," he said. "I couldn't let myself go. I didn't want to let go, but I did because I eventually found myself walking up toward that altar."

The pastor put his hands on Chuco's shoulders. All Chuco remembers was kneeling down. The next thing he knew, he was in another room, with people praying over him.

"They told me I was yelling and rolling around on the ground like a snake once that pastor prayed over me," he said. "I asked the pastor, 'What happened to me?' and he looked at me and said, 'My son, you've been delivered.'"

That was the beginning of a different set of struggles for Chuco. He had his addiction always looming over him, threatening his judgment and actions, and now he had the spirit of God trying to pull at him and make him clean.

"I joined the church and that time was the happiest time of my life," he remembered. "I was clean for almost two years. It was a miracle because no one had done to me what God did. I truly believe He touched my heart."

His involvement in New Harvest Church resulted in him serving as assistant pastor there. One day the head pastor said they needed someone to share God's word in another neighborhood and asked Chuco if he would go help. He didn't hesitate. He said yes and asked where the word of God was needed.

The pastor knew Chuco's past. "It's right in your old neighborhood," he said.

But gang life isn't about going to church. "It is against what our values are when you give your life to the neighborhood," said Chuco, "They tell you not to get involved in church. You don't get involved in anything but the gang."

When he went back, many of his homeboys were in prison or gone from the neighborhood. Other homeboys didn't seem to care he was in the church. He started leading and he felt good about what he was bringing to his neighborhood as he watched more and more homeboys fill the church. Despite this, he felt something was missing from his life. He couldn't figure out what it was, but the emptiness it caused started to leave a void.

"I felt something bad, deep inside me and didn't know who to talk to about it," he said. "I never learned to process anything or to heal from my past. I just kept burying my emotions and the Bible doesn't teach you how to deal with that. They tell you to 'Give it to God' or 'Pray to God,' but how can you do that without working through it too? No one could make me heal, so I started to feel worse and needed to numb myself from the pain, so I went right back to the only thing I remember that could make me feel good and far away from all the pain I kept inside... I went back to using heroin."

Chuco went back to his old ways. "I felt as if I was in a spiritual warfare with myself because God was trying to bring me back, but I fought it. I resisted until something bigger than me took place. Usually something big has to happen to make you change."

WHILE HE STRUGGLED and continued using, he was living with his parents, in their one-bedroom house. They knew he was using again, since he was gone at night and slept most of the day.

"I was using methadone every day and selling here and there to survive. I didn't rob or steal anymore because California had its Three Strikes Law, and I didn't want to end up in prison for life. So I mostly laid low, doing my thing.

"One day my brothers came over to the house and approached me. I'm drunk. They tell me they want me out of the house and to get my stuff and leave. They were forcing me to move on, and I'm thinking that's *not* how I'm going to leave— not like that. We started arguing and a fight broke out. My parents run into the room, and they are both fighting against me."

As things became more heated, Chuco reached into his pocket for his knife.

"I stabbed my brothers," he said, quietly. "Right in front of my mom and dad, I stabbed them. One of them almost died.

"All I remember was my mom screaming and it ringing in my ears as I took off running. I hid out at my girlfriend's house or somewhere, and I ended up getting arrested. I'm up for attempted murder. I'm now in jail, full of remorse and guilt.

"I had the chance to change and didn't. My mom was there, begging me to stop, and I didn't. I tore my whole family apart in an instant, and the worse thing for me was I was almost there, almost at my turning point. Now I was facing life in prison."

When his court day arrived, he was brought in and watched both of his brothers take the stand. They both testified that Chuco was only acting in self-defense. They said they had provoked him and that the knife was theirs and it was their fault, not his.

Instead of life in prison, he was sentenced to three years in prison. Chuco remembers it as the worst years of his life.

"I had so much shame and guilt. My cellmate would go to sleep and I would pray so that no one could hear me. I prayed for God to please help me," he said.

When he was released, he committed to changing his life, but started using again. "My hurt was so deep. I didn't know how to deal with it so I went back to the only way I knew how. At the same time, I knew I needed help."

He went to other homeboys in the neighborhood and started looking for Chuy because rumor had it he was in a program and doing alright. "I hadn't talked to him in years, and it took everything I had to dial his phone number.

"When I called him he immediately asked me if I was tired of living a life of using and I was like, 'Hold up homie, I just called you to see how you are.' And he went right back, 'You're calling me because you are tired of using.' I fought him on it a bit, but eventually I started listening. He started talking about detox programs and offered to help me get treatment and get clean.

"I only heard two words: detox and clean. That's what I wanted. My detox lasted 12 days and when I was done, for the first time in my life, I was out of jail and clean. Chuy found me at home after I was out and offered me more help, but I told

CHUCO WITH HIS BROTHER, LITTLE CHUCO, WITH *RANFLA*

him I was OK. I didn't realize then how he had gone through what I was going through and knew the temptations I would be facing."

And when temptation was there, Chuy was too, helping Chuco stay focused and clean. Chuy took him to his support meetings, even though Chuco was skeptical at first. "When I got there to those meetings, I saw seven guys I had done time with. And right by the door, I kid you not, there was one empty chair," he said. "That chair was for me."

Chuy eventually convinced Chuco to get treatment to stay clean. His first month there, he found what he had been missing when he was in church—the opportunity to heal. But Chuco wanted to be in charge of the group, to dominate them. "I started acting like I was in charge, going back to my old ways. They wanted to kick me out because of my attitude.

"One of the staffers, a big guy, came over and told me to

pack my shit and go... to get out. He said the only place an attitude like mine belonged was in jail. For the first time, I didn't fight him or yell. I just tucked my tail between my legs in anger and walked away. I had never done that in my life."

Four days later, Chuy approached Chuco again. He held out his hand and pulled Chuco close and said, "I want to tell you I love you. You're going to be OK. You beat your pride. You will get through this."

Chuco finished treatment and started working. "I hadn't had a real job in my entire life. An agency called me and offered me a part-time job in City of Commerce. I told my boss that I was an ex-convict and he still gave me a chance. One day he offered to drive me home, but I was nervous because I didn't want him to know I was living in Sober Living housing so I tried to get him to drop me off before we got there. He looked at me and said, 'I'm going to tell you something, but you cannot tell anyone in the company, but I live on the next block.'"

IN TIME, CHUCO WAS HIRED and still works at Cri-Help/ Socorro today as an intake supervisor for admissions, where he helps people dealing with substance abuse get the treatment they need to beat their addictions.

"I believe God placed me here," he said.

It's been 16 years since Chuco has used drugs. In addition, living in Norwalk with his wife, Rita, of 24 years, he has graduated with an associate's degree from East Los Angeles Community College and has taken classes at California State University, Los Angeles. He is also certified in Domestic Violence Prevention for the Los Angeles County Probation Department, where he serves as a master facilitator in the program.

In his free time, he gives back to his community by serving on the Board of Directors for the Lincoln Heights Chamber of Commerce, and by working with elected officials for the best interest of underserved communities.

In 2012, Chuco had one of the proudest moments of his life.

He took his parents with him to the Downtown Criminal Court Building in Los Angeles and had them with him when he received his Certificate of Rehabilitation.

"They were both crying because the only time they had ever been in court with me before was when I was being sentenced for something," he said.

Then in 2012, Chuco submitted all his paperwork to request a pardon from Governor Jerry Brown. In 2014, he received full clemency on his record.

"Receiving forgiveness for all the crimes I have done is huge for me," he said. "I have it hanging in my office and another copy hanging in my house."

Chuco has also worked to establish relationships with his four children, who are all grown and have struggled with various challenges and addictions.

"I wasn't there for them at all when they were little, hardly seeing them," he said. "But now, I am here for them and try to help them in whatever way that I can. I tell them as long as they are doing the right thing and making good choices, I will help them through what they are going through as best I can."

Together, him and Rita have 16 grandchildren. "Life has become beautiful and I'm enjoying every moment that I can with my family," he said.

"It took me so long to learn that I was given a false belief system when I was just a kid. I was told I was supposed to die for my neighborhood and no one told me otherwise, so it became everything.

"Looking at it now, my belief system was there long before that older homeboy was. It was the values, family morals, and work ethic of my parents, whether it was my dad working in the fields or my mom making tortillas.

"I just didn't see it then and I didn't know how to break away from who I thought I was. I can only thank God for my life and the good parts of this journey of mine. We all go through things in this life. I'm just thankful and grateful I am here to talk about it."

TONITO WITH HIS WIFE TERRY, LATE 1980S

Antonio "Tonito" Fierro

"WOULD YOU LIKE ANYTHING TO DRINK, SIR?"

Three friends sat at a table when the waiter approached.

Jesse Olivas ordered and his wife, Raquel, did too. "Two cokes, please."

The waiter paused and started to walk away.

"Hey man," said the third person, his voice rising, "What, do you not see me here? Why don't you ask me what I want?"

Jesse tried to calm his friend down.

"It's OK, it's OK," Jesse said. "He didn't mean to skip you. Here tell him what you want."

Anthony "Tonito" Fierro put his order in and the rest of dinner went well.

On the way home, Raquel asked Jesse why Tonito had reacted so strongly.

Jesse had been thinking about the same thing. He thought of how young Tonito was when he started drinking and doing drugs. How he was found guilty of murder at 13. How he had no parents to raise him and how prison life was the only influence he had while he grew from boy to man.

"I don't know, baby," he said. "He's been locked up a long time. Sometimes this makes it so you don't know how to be."

Tonito grew up in Rosemead, where he lived with his mother, Vyrle, a heroin addict. The house always had different people in it, doing drugs and drinking.

"I used to steal beer out of the fridge and sneak it in the backyard to drink with my friends," Tonito remembered. "She never noticed. I knew she wouldn't."

He was 9.

Seeing that Tonito needed better influences, his Tio Joe started spending time with him. He even helped enroll him into sports. Tonito started playing soccer and baseball. He started to show a natural talent with baseball and enjoyed the praise he received from his coach and fellow teammates.

But by the age of 13, while in middle school, he started noticing gang members. He liked their tough attitudes, the way they dressed...something in him wanted to look that way, be that way. His mother was not sober enough to redirect him, and in little time, the excitement of hitting a homerun for his team dulled when compared to the thrill of breaking laws, fighting, and living *La Vida Loca.*

At 13, he was jumped into the Lomas gang. "They beat me into the *klika* at a park," he remembered. Shortly after, he started getting into more trouble and going to school less.

"I was smoking weed a lot," he said. "I also started breaking into houses to get the money to pay for the weed. I broke into all my neighbor's homes because I knew when they were home and when they weren't."

He started getting arrested and his mother became bothered with having to deal with him. She decided to send him to Los Angeles to live with his father, Anthony Sr., who was also addicted to heroin.

Anthony Sr. was an active gang member in Primera Flats. He was so happy to have his son around that he decided to let him do whatever he wanted. He sent him to school, but since the gang members there knew Tonito's dad as "Sleepy" and respected him, they did not bother him. They accepted him.

"I got worse over there," he said. "My dad was more like my friend instead of a parent. I stopped going to school and started stealing cars, breaking into factories. I went wild."

One night, Tonito and another guy from Primera Flats broke into a house and stole nearly $4,000. With the money, Tonito bought himself a car. At 13, he was cruising in his own car in East L.A. with no one to tell him "no" to anything.

His grandmother (Anthony Sr.'s mother) started to see how out-of-control her grandson was. She called Tonito's mother and told her she needed to take him back. She agreed, but mainly because she knew Tonito had a car and wanted it. He returned to Rosemead, but was on his own. His siblings were either older or much younger than him and his mother was in her own world... the only place he felt he belonged was with the homies.

ONE EVENING, 13-year-old Tonito and one of his homeboys drove back to Primera Flats and met up with another older homie, who had just stolen a car. They started driving through neighborhoods together, stopping and burglarizing homes. In one home, they found a gun.

"Once we had the gun, we wanted to rob a store," he remembered. "We found a little market and the guy from Flats told me to stay in the car waiting to take off while he and the other guy went into the store. So, I'm in the driver's seat at night, waiting for them to rob the store. Looking back, I think, man, I was just a kid."

At the time though, Tonito felt as fearless as any man. He waited and watched the rear view mirror for his friends, ready to hit the gas. In the silence of the night, gunshots rang out. He turned the ignition, ready.

"I remember seeing one of my friends run out," he said. "The store owner was chasing him. My friend was shooting at the man and the man was shooting back. He jumped in the car, and I floored it. The windows to the car were all shattering as he kept shooting at us."

Tonito had not felt an adrenaline rush like that before. After they drove a distance, the homie told Tonito he had shot a woman in the store. They immediately dumped the car and found themselves telling Anthony Sr. what had happened.

Three days later, Tonito was arrested. The friend that did not make it out had ratted and all three were now in jail. Both his friends were 18. Since no witnesses could identify for sure who killed the woman, the two homeboys faced the death penalty if either was found guilty.

Tonito, at 13, was a juvenile. It was 1980. The most time he could serve would be seven years.

"I made the decision to say I did it," he said. "I didn't do it, but I also didn't care. At that point, I was getting arrested, my parents were picking me up and I would do whatever I wanted again. What could happen to me? I wanted to know what it was like to do real time, so I was charged with robbery and murder and they sent me to youth authority."

HE MADE PAROLE IN THREE YEARS. He was back in Rosemead before his 18th birthday. Most of his time was spent partying and getting high. He preferred smoking PCP. It was not long before he was gangbanging again.

"I would borrow a homie's gun and go shoot up houses, do drive-bys in San Gabriel," he said. "I wasn't doing it because I was angry at anything. I just wanted to be seen as bad. I wanted the other homies to talk about what I was doing and get my name out there."

Up until this point, Tonito had never tried heroin. He saw both his parents use it regularly and felt that he wanted to keep his distance from it. One night though, a friend of his was smoking PCP with him and then told him she wanted to get loaded. She thought Tonito had done heroin and offered him some. He rejected it, but felt curious as she went to the bathroom to shoot up. He followed her and told her he would do it with her.

"I put my arm out and she injected it into me and I felt this rush from my feet coming up to my body," he said. "Then I blacked out and it took me awhile to come back," he said.

The next week he told a friend about what happened. The friend told Tonito he could have died—that the girl gave him too much for his first time. And that if he had not smoked the PCP, he would have died.

"She thought I had done heroin before, so she hit me hard," he said. "She didn't know it was my first time."

During this time, he was still living with his mother. She would send him out to buy her drugs. Within a year, he was back in jail on a parole violation. He was sent to fire camp. One of the guys had a pass to go off grounds. When the guy returned, he brought alcohol and Tonito drank with him. When they were found drunk, camp officials decided to transfer Tonito to Preston Youth Authority in Northern California. Once at Preston, his one-year sentence turned into three years as he participated in race riots there.

As his 21st birthday approached, Tonito knew he would be released soon. "They had to let me go," he said. "And when they did, I just went back to my old ways. I was just partying and getting high all the time."

Once he was out, he would go back and forth from Rosemead to Los Angeles. He met Terry, now his wife, in L.A. They got together and he soon moved in with her in her mother's house.

He did not have his own car, so he stole cars for his transportation. He was working, but spending his money on partying and drugs. One night, he was caught in a stolen car and was going back to prison, but his boss wrote him a letter and he ended up getting one year, but with a work furlough, meaning he would spend his days working and his nights in jail.

"When I was three months into my sentence, I wanted heroin, I had been bringing it in with me when I could, so I was addicted by then. I hadn't had a hit so I was sick from withdrawals. Instead of going to work, I went to the neighborhood to get some. When I got there, I got loaded and started partying and drinking. When I realized the time and that I had to get back, I asked my homies to give me a ride."

They came to pick him up in a stolen car. Tonito insisted on driving and he was pulled over. "We weren't even a block from there and the cops came up and tried to pull us over. I didn't want to get caught like that, so I took them on a little chase."

He was sentenced to prison for it. Two years.

"I was 22 years old," he said. "I was being sent to San Quentin. It was my first time going to adult prison. I wasn't scared... nothing. I didn't even stop to realize how good I had it—serving one year with a job and a work furlough and how one day I just fucked it all up."

He was a newlywed during this time. He and Terry had been married two months.

In San Quentin there were a lot of race riots. During one, a guy was stabbed. Tonito had been there two months. Tonito and six other guys were pulled in to determine who did it.

"I didn't do it, but no one knew who did it," he said. "The guy didn't die, but was hurt bad. They sent me to Pelican Bay for 18 months as a result. They put me in the SHU Program (Security Housing Unit), which means they put me in isolation."

Tonito was in the SHU Program for nearly a year. Once it was over, they sent him to New Folsom, where he stayed an additional six months. Once his two years were served, he was released.

He moved back in with his wife. She soon became pregnant. In 1992, Tonito's son, Anthony Jr., was born. He had been out of prison one year.

One day, some homies were drinking with Tonito on his front porch, while his one-week-old baby and wife slept inside. His friends decided to rob some guys who walked by. Tonito did not participate, but asked them to do it down the block instead of in front of his house.

After his homies robbed the guys, they went back to Tonito's porch. Shortly after, the cops rolled up with the guys in the back of their cruiser, looking for who robbed them. Tonito was arrested.

"They charged me with robbery," he said. "They wanted me to plea to get less time, but I didn't do it, so I wouldn't plea. Anyway, the lawyer told me I'd get 15 years if I went to trial and was found guilty—or eight years if I pleaded guilty. I was sure the jury would not blame me for something I didn't do. I wanted the trial."

"The guys who were robbed could not see who did it since the robber came from behind. They only saw a bunch of tattoos on someone's arms. The prosecutor asked me to show my arms, which have tattoos. Bam, I was guilty—just like that."

Tonito was sentenced to five years. While in prison, Vyrle, his mother, died from cancer. It did not affect Tonito since he hardly had a relationship with her due to her addiction.

"When I got out my son was a little boy," he remembered. "I remember feeling so happy when we brought him home, but I didn't get to spend much time with him."

He started using speed and not spending much time at home. "I loved my son, you know, but I just didn't care about anything so I wouldn't go and be with my family. The speed just kept me out."

Terry became pregnant again, but Tonito does not remember most of her pregnancy because he started using heroin with his father again during that time.

While she was pregnant, Tonito had an affair with a woman who lived in his cousin's apartment complex, where he spent a lot of time. His wife found out and told him to stop the relationship or she would leave him.

"I loved her and once she said she would leave," he remembered, "I knew I had to do whatever she said to have her stay. I ended the relationship."

The mistress, however, decided to approach Tonito's wife and told her the relationship was still happening, even though it no longer was.

Terry was furious and confronted Tonito. He promised her it was over. In anger, he went to the other woman's apartment, kicked in the door, and yelled at her to leave his wife and his marriage alone.

Once he left, the woman called the police and told them Tonito had beaten her. Her roommate confirmed the story. Tonito was arrested again for "terrorist threats" and was facing his third felony strike, which would get him a sentence of 25-years-to-life.

"I didn't touch her," he said. "They had me sitting in jail for six months. When my daughter was born, I wasn't there. Then suddenly the girl and her roommate had a falling out and the 'witness' wanted to take her story back.

"I ended up getting charged with trespassing and already served the time waiting for this all to unfold."

When he was released, instead of going home to see his wife, young son, and new baby girl, he went to his father's apartment and got high.

"I stayed out like that for about six months, getting high and not being around," he said.

One day, a supermarket manager he knew, offered him a job. He took it and started working. He stopped using heroin and started using methadone.

"All I did was work and go home," he said. "I even got my wife pregnant one more time," he smiles. "Another boy."

He started saving money. They moved into their own place in 1998. Everything seemed to be going well until 2000 when his house was raided. He had been on parole and did not know it. His parole officer had retired and did not close his file.

He was sentenced to 90 days in jail. When he got out, he no longer had a job, no income, and the foundation they had built was gone. He soon went back to his old ways of using heroin. Then, he started selling it to support his addiction.

One morning, while selling heroin, he was caught and arrested. The cops found 17 bags of heroin in his house.

"My kids saw so much," he said. "I think about that now.

TONITO WITH LOMAS FRIENDS.

How they must have felt seeing their house get raided and their dad arrested."

He was sentenced to less than three years. When he was released, his wife and kids were living in another house. Tonito continued getting high and soon had another possession case thrown on him. Two more years sentenced and another two years served.

In 2005, he was out of prison, but still getting high with his father. He was able to stay out of trouble for a while and decided to move the family out of Los Angeles and closer to Alhambra.

In 2011, he was caught with another possession. This time though, the judge gave him a drug outpatient program for one year.

"My parole officer said I needed an inpatient program, where I had to stay in the facility to get clean," he said. "He

TONITO WITH DAUGHTER AND GRANDCHILDREN.

pushed for it, but there wasn't room for me. So, I started the outpatient program, which meant I had freedom, which meant I was still using.

"I would go to my classes high. I would alter my drug tests. I had a 30-day progress report and I went to my parole officer and told him that I was submitting dirty tests.

"When the judge found out, he was ready to send me to jail instead of back to the program. My parole officer went privately to the judge and told him I needed an inpatient program. I was already handcuffed and about to get on the bus to the county jail when they stopped me. They told me I was going to an inpatient program instead."

TONITO HAD NOT THOUGHT of drug recovery programs before, nor had he thought they could change him. "I thought I would die high—not from an overdose or anything, but almost like it was always going to be a part of my life," he said.

The day that Tonito left the courthouse was the last day he ever used drugs. The date was September 19, 2012. He completed his recovery program at the Walden House in El Monte. He was off parole in March 2015.

As he remains committed to his recovery and sobriety, his life now revolves around his two grandsons, Joseph, 4, and Andrew, 2.

"When I would get high, my daughter did not trust me with her boys," he said, emotionally. "She did not want me to spend a lot of time with them, but now, they are in my life and I am in theirs. They call their father 'daddy' and me 'dad.' There is nothing better."

His two sons are struggling with their own issues with drug addiction. One son is currently in jail and the other lives at home with Terry.

In 2013, while still on probation, Tonito went to visit Anthony Jr., his son who is a gang member. They were driving home together and were pulled over. The police officer arrested Tonito on a parole violation for associating with a gang member. He tried to argue that he was just spending time with his son, but was still arrested. The officer told him he would be out in 10 days. He was held for 60 days.

"The police officer didn't write in the report I was with my son," he said. "So I stayed two months."

Tonito realized that to stay clean, he needed to distance himself from his sons and their choices and work on himself. He currently lives in a men's recovery home. He and Terry are still married. He also works for a friend's cleaning business.

"I'm 48-years-old and last year I barely got my driver's license. I have a truck I bought that is in my own name. These are things I never imagined having.

"I don't think I will ever get high again with God's help because I know what it takes for me and how far I have come," he said. "I don't want to be away from my grandkids. I know I wasn't there to see my kids grow up. Right now, my grandson plays T-ball and soccer, and I am at every game. When I see those kids, they light me up.

"I thank God for everything I have right now."

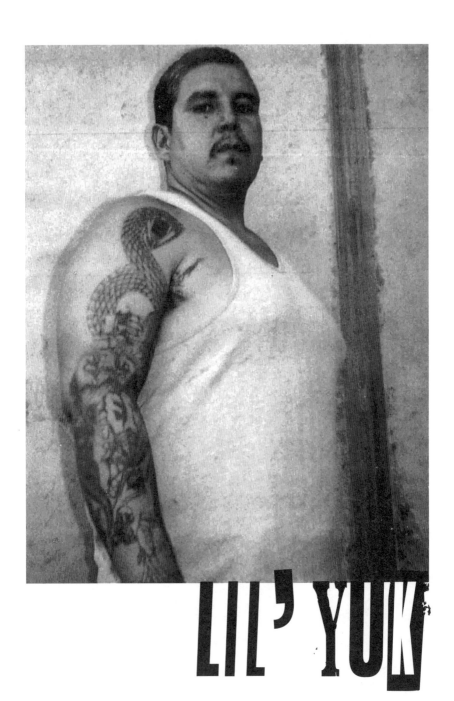

LIL' YUK

Jess "Lil' Yuk" Montecino

THE GLARE FROM THE SUN made it difficult to see through his car's windshield. Jess Montecino squinted, but pushed his foot heavier on the gas pedal, accelerating. He was headed south over the Grapevine to Montebello. The car's speed raced along with his heartbeat. A thousand thoughts went through his mind.

Is my son OK? Will he live?

He knew Jess Jr. had been shot. His ex-wife, Elena, had called him, frantic, and he tried to replay what she said to him while he drove.

Elena told him that Jess Jr. had been shot in the face. He knew his 17-year-old son was a part of the 213 Gang in Montebello and things had been heating up, but he did not expect this. He wanted to know who did it. He felt a combination of worry and rage.

At that moment, a white dove slammed against his windshield, startling him and shaking his thoughts. He looked at his speedometer—he was going nearly 110 mph. At that moment, his cell rang.

It was Rammy, his friend and sponsor, who had helped him recover from his addictions. He had somehow already learned of the news.

"Jess, Jess," he said. "Listen to me. You need to slow down."

Rammy had friends in Montebello and had asked them to check on Jess Jr.'s status at the hospital. He did not have much information, only that doctors thought his son would be OK.

That was all Jess needed to hear. His only son would be all right. He kept driving and prayed that what Rammy had heard was true.

When he arrived at General Hospital in Los Angeles, Jess ran in and saw that his closest friends were already there— Cecil, Mike, and Louie. They embraced him and stood by him while the doctors explained what had happened.

The bullet went into his son's left underarm, came out of his shoulder, went back into his neck and exited through his right eye. Doctors could not believe that the bullet missed any vital organs. Jess Jr. would never see out of that eye again, but he would live. Those were the only words that mattered.

Jess and his friends stayed at the hospital while his son slowly recovered. No words were spoken among the men to explain what had happened. No words were needed. They all knew firsthand how *la vida loca* worked and how easily it could nearly kill a 17-year-old kid. After all, they had all been South San Gabriel Lomas gang members themselves.

JESS "LIL' YUK" MONTECINO was born in East Los Angeles, but moved to South San Gabriel at the age of 9. Raised by loving parents and five siblings, Jess believed he had a good childhood. He remembered the sense of community he experienced growing up in East Los. In fact, his neighbors would bring their kids to play with Jess and his siblings regularly.

"When we moved to South San Gabriel, we were moving to the home of the *cholo*," he said. "I immediately felt pulled in and I knew I wanted to follow that image."

By 10, Jess started drinking with one of his uncles. His older brother was already involved with Lomas and he admired that. By his early teenage years, his uncle introduced him to selling drugs, which eventually led to him using. Being so young, Jess found himself just wanting to follow them, be like them.

"The older homeboys were respected," he said. "They were the ones who had the nice cars and the girlfriends. They were

LIL' YUK WITH HIS SON, JESS, JR.

the ones no one messed with. We all wanted to be like those guys.

"We were taught that we had to be able to take a good ass kicking to be like them and the more you did, the more you were respected."

Jesús, Jess' dad, was his best friend. Born in Mexico, Jesús was never involved in any gangs, but was street smart and expected his son to be accountable for his actions.

"I never went to juvenile hall," said Jess. "I think it is because my dad was always there for me. He saw me getting more involved in the neighborhood and tried to tell me not to get so caught up in it, but I wouldn't listen. Kids don't listen to their parents. I think he was the reason I never went to juvie. Anytime I would get busted, he was there to pick me up. For many, the cops were the only ones to pick them up."

Jesús was a believer in tough love. Once, Jess was accused of stealing shotguns from a cop's patrol car. While at a friend's house, Jess' house was raided by police. When Jess saw the police cars in front of his house, he did not go home. The next morning, when he went in, his dad was there.

"He told me to take a shower. Afterward, he asked me what I had done to make the cops raid the house. I told him I hadn't done anything. He said, 'OK, if you have nothing to hide, you go tell the cops that.'"

They drove together to the police. His dad explained that he could not have the police raiding his home with Delores, Jess' mother, and his siblings there. When they arrived, Jesús introduced Jess to a police officer and offered to let him be questioned.

"You better not put any marks on my son," he told the officer. "I will wait right here for him."

Turned out the police did not have any evidence linking to Jess. He went home with his father. He still remembers what his dad told him on the way home.

"In our family, if you do something wrong, you own it."

By 14, Lomas members initiated Jess, again by a ritual beating. He had been involved with the neighborhood for some time already, but getting jumped in made it official.

It happened at school. "One of the homeboys came up to me when I was going to class and told me that my brother told them I was getting into the neighborhood that day," he remembered. "I got lucky. There were only three guys and I looked at them and thought, 'Man, these guys got nothing,' and I went in hard. That was my little initiation."

With two sons in Lomas, Jesús was not pleased, but realized he could do nothing to make his boys stop their gang life. Jess started gangbanging, using more drugs and fighting for the neighborhood.

Shortly after his 18th birthday, Jess found himself spending more and more time in the county jail.

"I did a lot of county time," he said. "I would be there a year or two and then come out for six months and I was going right back to the lifestyle that put me in county jail in the first place."

Jess mostly robbed liquor stores for money and to feed his addictions. He first tried heroin in his early 20s while in jail.

HOMIES IN CHINO PRISON, 1970S.

In 1984, he was sent to prison in Chino. He stayed there for two years and then went on to parole.

"Looking back, my dad tried to stop me," he said. "And most people look at gang members and they think, 'If people had a family or a wife, they wouldn't do such things.' But I had that stuff—I had the car, the family, the wife.

"In fact, one time, my dad told my girl, 'See where Jess will be during Christmas; he will go to jail because it's cheaper than buying presents.' And you know what? Even though I had my wife and son... that was true. Come Christmas time, no one asked where I was. I was in jail."

In January 1995, Jess was in a heated argument with Elena. At one point, she called 911. Jess was so infuriated he went up to her to suck on her face, to leave a mark. He was so loaded on drugs, he found himself biting her, leaving marks on her face.

"I never hit her," he said. "But doing that landed me 10 years in Centinela prison. I served a little over eight years. My son was only 2-years-old when I got in. He was 11 when I got out."

The time didn't intimidate Jess. "By that time, going to prison felt more like a game. In fact, since I knew I was doing a long stretch, I proposed to her before I went in, and we got married."

Their marriage did not last. Once he was out and decided to leave her, Elena gave Jess Jr. to him.

The responsibility felt good to Jess. After he served his time, he searched for a job. Soon after, he was hired and was able to purchase a car. He would go and watch his son play baseball and tried to build a relationship with him.

"I remember when I first got out, his godmother took me to see him," he remembered. "He was in a little baseball uniform and he was so happy to see me."

In time Jess felt overwhelmed with the idea of raising his son. During this time, he was also struggling with his addiction to heroin and his son witnessed the worst of it.

"I was doing five or six spoons a day," he said. "He and I were living in my homeboy's washroom at that point. I remember praying to God for a dry up. The only way I knew to do this was to go to jail to dry out. I knew that programs existed to help get over drug addiction, but they were the furthest thing from my mind at that point."

His prayer came true. He was soon sentenced to 90 days for possession of an illegal switchblade, which was actually a broken buck knife, but he knew it was a chance to dry out. When he was released, he went back to living with his son.

However, when Jess Jr. was 11-years-old, Jess noticed drugs missing from his chest of drawers.

"At first he tried to tell me he had taken it to school to show it off," Jess said. "I didn't want to think he was using."

Jess continued to struggle with the demons of his addiction. He would party and get high with his friends and ask Jess Jr. to drive him home.

"We would get so loaded, I would let him drive so I wouldn't be the drunk driver," he said. "He was like 12 when I had him do this. I know now that what I was doing was child endangerment, but I wasn't in the right state of mind to know the difference."

His son's adolescent years were spent watching his dad

struggle with his addiction. During this same time, Jess' mother moved to Bakersfield and Jess decided it would be better for him and his son to move to the Central Valley to live with her.

Jess knew that he needed help. He called his homeboy Chuco, who worked at a rehabilitation program, for help. He started detox on December 15, 2005 and has remained clean since. Living and working as a furniture mover in Bakersfield, Jess remained committed to his sobriety and started trying to help his son, who had started to get more involved with gang life in Montebello.

"When I came home from the program, Jess Jr. was 14 and he had a girlfriend. He wanted my car. He wanted to go down the Grapevine to hang with his homies in Montebello. He took my car to go there," Jess said. "Finally, I told him if he wanted to stay down there, he should just stay down there, but I still brought him back up to Bakersfield and he kept taking my car."

Jess Jr. also started getting into more trouble during this

time, getting arrested for fighting and ending up in juvenile hall. Jess went back to recovery and lived in the program's housing facility for six months. When he went home, his son had already established himself in the 213 Gang and was full of tattoos.

"It all happened so fast—losing control of him," Jess remembered. "The gang liked him because he wasn't afraid of anything. I taught him to be that way... I taught him to fight. I used to hit him and he could take my punches."

WHEN HE WAS SHOT, Jess struggled with how to react. Relieved that his son would live, he still felt anger over what happened.

"I stayed at the hospital for two weeks," he said. "I was afraid to leave. I felt if I left, I risked losing him. The hardest part for me was not retaliating. I grew up being taught that if someone does something bad to you, you do something twice as bad to them. That was our lifestyle. I know that if I wanted to, I could have found out who did this to my son, but I didn't."

Jess Jr. spent his 18th birthday in the hospital, recovering from the shooting. The day he was to be released to go home, the police came and arrested him.

"It hurt me so much when they did that," Jess remembered, his voice cracking. "There was nothing I could do to stop them.

"They arrested him because they wanted to question him about another incident. They accused my son of doing something, he denied it, and they told him they would keep him until he confessed. Next thing you know, the cops put cases on him and he gets 16 years."

Jess hopes that his son is able to pull himself from gang and drug life faster than he did. "I pray for God to touch his heart," he said. "I want him to know that there is a life outside of the life he knows. It took me too long to find it. I never thought I would leave the neighborhood. I thought I would get life in prison or die on the streets—that was my destiny."

"I never thought I would be someone with a bank account, a car, or a full-time job. I never would imagine paying bills or having vacation time. I want my son to know it's possible. He is young... he has so much to learn."

Jess still resides in Bakersfield with his wife Monica, where he is fulfilling the promise he made to his father (now deceased) to take care of his mother. Jess visits his son in prison often. In addition to working, he volunteers with the Kern County's Narcotics Anonymous Program, where he spends time helping people recover from their addictions.

CHINO

Mike "Chino" Moreno

THE YEAR WAS 1982. It was a Saturday night and all the army boys were ready to party with the locals in Northern California. Instead of ironing their uniforms perfectly, the Latino soldiers pleated their pinstripes and starched their shirt collars. All the local girls from Salinas liked army boys, and Mike Moreno wanted to look his best.

Held at a local hall, the music blared and the room was full of people. The large moon that night tried to remind everyone how late the time was, but no one bothered to pay attention. A fight had started.

Mike, a young 21-year-old, was drawn like a moth to a flame to the conflict. He saw his army partner and a guy from his local neighborhood argue, and then break into a full-blown fight. Something flickered in the dark room, like a mirror. The lights from the party reflected against it, burning Mike's eyes. He switched his attention to the local's face and knew the blade was no bluff. He had to help his friend.

He leapt and grabbed the local to stop him. Out of nowhere, another local stuck a gun in his face and pulled the trigger, shooting twice, but missing both times. The party that had minutes before been a whirlwind of laughter and loud music had cleared, and in the emptiness of the hall, time appeared to stand still.

Mike looked around him, but the locals were gone. His friend was slumped over on the ground. He reached over to him to touch him and tell him that the fight was over, but he had no words. He could not speak. At that moment, his sight dominated his other senses as it took in the red blood that was pouring the very life out of his friend.

He knew his friend was dying. He cradled him and counted numerous stab wounds confirming the blade was swung not in threat, but in promise. Mike felt his friend's breathing grow faint and then stop. At the same time, he felt himself go numb.

"Sometimes, I wish I could just forget that night," he said, nearly two decades later. "Understanding life and death is different for everyone. For me, I saw it when I got home that night and changed. My homeboy's blood soaked through my pants, into my underwear, I even had it in my socks.

"I tripped out about that night for awhile, but decided not to talk about it or think about it. I just did not want it to faze me like I knew it could."

THAT DARK NIGHT was not the first time Mike Moreno had tested fate, his own or anyone else's. His story is rooted just blocks east of downtown, in Boyle Heights, where he was the middle child among four siblings.

As a little boy he found amusement with his friends in vacant lots they would explore together. There they would have rock fights against each other, catch tarantulas and torture them with ants, or harass the hobos for fun.

His house on Winter Street was meager. Its one bedroom resulted in nothing more than cramped tension held together by four walls. Jimmy, Mike's father, was an alcoholic and had no problem subjecting his violent temper on Mary, his mother, or on him or any of his siblings.

His anger started forming early. As a young child, he tried to push the feeling deep within himself, but every time his mother was abused, he could feel it pump harder and hotter in his veins.

"She couldn't leave him, you know?" he said. "What would she do? Where would she go with five kids? It was different back then. You just had to make it work, and that's what she was trying to do."

In 1969, the family decided to move further east to Rosemead. Both Jimmy and Mary felt the move would be better for their kids, but as soon as they arrived, Mike could see "that place was just as crazy as East Los."

Within months of the move, Mike began hanging out with homeboys from the neighborhood. At 13, he took his first hit of heroin from his older homeboy, Chuy. As the warm rush flowed through his veins, he liked the calming peace the drug brought him, and he soon became addicted. Around the same time, he lost his virginity to his babysitter, "an older woman," who he described as someone who simply "showed me what to do."

While he was exploring with drugs, sex and alcohol, things at home grew worse. His father,

1982, CHINO AT FORT ORD.

who had worked 15 years as a grocery clerk, grew ill and stopped working. Jimmy stayed in his room for hours, days, and then weeks at a time. But Mike never asked questions as to what was wrong with his father. With the help of drugs, it was almost as if Mike was able to disconnect himself from his surroundings. As time went on, the family discovered that Jimmy was mentally ill, and with that diagnosis came a stigma or shame often attached to mental illness. Doctors prescribed medication and electrical shock treatments to help Mike's father sleep, and sometimes he did for days at a time.

When Jimmy was awake and around the kids, things were not any better. The beatings continued and Mike opted to be defiant instead of cower away as his siblings did. This only resulted in harsher beatings, sometimes so bad he was not able to move afterward.

"Now that he's dead, I don't think I have any bitterness or resentment toward him," he said. "I mean, he was sick. When I really try, I can remember times when he was funny. When I was going through a bad time, he would tell me that the stuff I was on was going to be my demise. Looking back, I can also remember him telling me he was proud of me, that he thought I turned out pretty good despite the obstacles I had endured.

"He knew he created anger in me and he admitted it," Mike recalled. "Except the thing was, whenever I was angry I went to drugs and alcohol."

AT SCHOOL, Mike's problems at home along with his drug use were beginning to take their toll not only on his grades, but also on any teachers' tolerance to keep him in their classrooms.

Not able to read or write at the age of 12, he found himself embarrassed in the classroom whenever he was called on or asked a question, so he began acting out and misbehaving to avoid anyone knowing the truth behind his illiteracy.

"The teachers started putting me in what was called the 'Opportunity Room,' which was the room for the crazy kids," he said. "I was there because I was labeled 'disruptive.' I told them all to 'fuck off' when I got there just so they knew not to mess with me.

"I was a Napoleon Kid and had a lot of anger," he said. "I would purposely pick fights with bigger guys. One time, a big kid was picking on my best friend, so when he got off the bus, I picked up a rock and started hitting him with it. Before you know it, counselors and teachers were chasing me. Another time, a teacher tried to take me to the counselor's office, and I tried to jump out of a window. They used to hit you back then for punishment. I used to get beat at home; I was not going to let teachers hit me too. I would run away from them. I always felt like I had to run, always running."

In between suspensions, he spent more and more time away from home and soon decided to continue this trend and run away from home altogether. He had two friends, who were sisters. He decided to sneak into their home and stay. There he slept in their walk-in closet.

"I was a cute and funny kid," he said. "So my friends would hide me. I'd always be within two-to-three miles from my house though. I remember hearing my grandma a few times looking for me, calling out my name in the neighborhood."

One of the sisters, Rosie, gave Mike his first tattoo, "Chino," which was his nickname. Over the years, he allowed his body to become a canvas for a variety of ink, which ranged from gang affiliations to Aztec warriors. Countless hours of artwork call his skin home. By wearing a dress shirt, the majority of his tattoos can be covered.

"Each tattoo tells a story about my life, my history, my culture," he said. "They all mean something to me."

Since he was staying in the neighborhood, Mike began affiliating himself with the Pico Nuevo gang. Soon, he found himself ditching school more often, and the few times he was there, he was normally in trouble. Between the school district and the court, it was decided that he was guilty of being an "incorrigible" youth, one who was "incapable of being corrected or reformed." As a result of this judgment for his numerous issues in school and at home, any time he would act up or get in trouble, he would be sentenced to time in juvenile hall.

His first day in juvenile hall, he was 13. That place would serve as his second home until his 17th birthday. Mike learned a lot during his time in youth corrections. He started growing up and making friends, he finally learned to read and write while there, and at one point even earned his learner's permit to drive. In placement, he finally found a school, a sense of structure that suited him.

"I had an odd yet comforting sense of belonging while in placement," he remembered. "I did better with the schedule, the routine there. I think everyone does better with a sense of discipline and structure, be it in a prep school, the military or even prison.

"There were times when I was truly homesick," he said. "But once I was back at home and saw all the problems that were still there, I couldn't figure out what it was that I thought I was missing."

Mike adapted quickly to being in placement. Whenever he acted out, he was locked up or punished. Soon, he started connecting his actions to his consequences.

"I tried to hang out with the older crowds," he said. "At 13, I would run around with older homeboys, some who were 25-years-old. I used to get scared sometimes, especially with riots or things like that. I never knew what would happen."

Using that logic, at 15 and still in juvenile hall, Mike decided he needed to be able to protect himself in case something did happen to him. He asked around for help, and soon he learned how to make his first shank out of his toothbrush.

When he was out of placement, he tried to have a normal teenage life. He would find ways to get rides with his friends to cruise down Whittier Boulevard. Whenever he could he would flirt with girls and even try to convince them to be his girl-friends. Sometimes while locked up, he would even invite them to any events or co-ed dances the juvenile hall held, and make out with them in any dark corner that allowed.

Despite his interaction with girls, he never knew what it was like to walk a girlfriend of his to class or to hold her books. Due to his time in juvenile hall, he never fully experienced courtship or the innocent, intimate things others experienced at his age.

"Things like prom and homecoming dances," he said. "I had no idea what those things were or why they were so important."

In juvenile hall, Gilbert Duran introduced himself to Mike and asked him where he was from. Mike told him Pico Nuevo.

Gilbert said he was from Lomas, a gang in Rosemead. Mike started thinking that since he was from there, that he was really more Lomas than he was Pico Nuevo.

ONE WEEKEND, WHILE HOME, Mike was jumped into Lomas in front of Mark Keppel High School in Alhambra. Fighting his way through, Mike jumped up to hit one of the guys and missed, hitting a brick wall instead. He heard a snap, and realized he had broken his arm.

"I didn't volunteer to be in a gang in my life," he said. "I was jumped in, and once that happens, you don't go back."

As a result of fighting, Mike was arrested. He was late returning to juvenile hall, which resulted in him being confined. The only thing on Mike's mind was going home for Christmas, which was approaching at that time. He was told he would not be able to get a pass to go home because of his fighting.

"They decided to take me to another facility," he recalled. "I

CHINO AT FORT BRAGG, 82ND AIRBORNE DIVISION, 1979.

tried to stab a counselor before we left, and then I tried to jump out of the car on the way. I was so angry they were telling me I could not be home for Christmas."

When Mike was out of juvenile hall at 17, his probation officer encouraged him to join the military. He had no other plans for his life, so he enlisted in the army. Since the early 80s were considered peaceful times, Mike traveled and trained with the army and visited various U.S. states and Panama. He proudly served as part of the 82nd Airborne Division.

"The army gave me some great memories," Mike said. "I worked hard. I even jumped out of airplanes. My whole life, I was afraid of heights, and when I jumped out of a plane for the first time, I felt like I was proving something to someone. I remember my Uncle Anthony telling me I did not have the courage to join, and I did it. I've always been like that. I want to prove I can do the things no one thinks I can."

Like juvenile hall, Mike benefited from the structure and discipline the army offered. His last year there, though, involved more than army drills and training as Mike began to use heroin more and more.

"I got caught up in my old ways," he said. "The army was like a 9 to 5 job back then. I would be a soldier during that time and then be a party animal afterward. I started hanging out with the same guys. We almost became a gang in the army. When we went into the towns or whatever afterward, we made that known to the locals. We were always packing, and they knew it."

That dark night was a result of the gang and drug use Mike experienced in the army. The army never reprimanded him for any wrongdoing. After serving five years, he was honorably discharged. At 23, he again was on his way home.

He moved to Boyle Heights, where his family had returned, and started working as a custodian for L.A. Unified School District. At the same time, he worked part-time as a bouncer for the Quiet Canyon Nightclub in Montebello.

HE SOON MET AND MARRIED BERTHA. Together, they had a son, Mikey. Describing himself as "too young" for the responsibility of having a family, Mike grew restless. He started shooting up heroin again regularly and found excuses to go out and party instead of stay home with his family. Soon, Mike was in county jail after one too many DUIs and assault violations.

"She came from a good family," he said, describing his wife. "I came from the opposite. See, my mom stood by my dad even when he would beat her, when he would drink... and I always thought that's how it was with women. A man could treat her like dirt, and if she was a good woman she'd stay by you. I know now that that is wrong, but I grew up seeing that—so that's how I treated the women in my relationships."

When their son was nearly 2-years-old, Mike discovered his wife was having an affair. He caught her at home with another man. The anger he knew as a child had never left him, the distrust and attachment issues were still there. The only thing he knew was that he wanted her out of his house and his life.

"Looking back, I can see that I being on the streets or in jail hurt her," he said. "But she cheated on me. I know two wrongs don't make a right, but I could not forgive her. I know my son missed out on a family life because of us, his parents.

"Sometimes, I think if I would have just been a hard working and faithful man that we probably would have lasted."

Despite the divorce, Bertha never gave Mike a hard time when it came to visiting little Mikey. Even though the separation was something he insisted, Mike had a hard time adjusting to not having his wife in his life.

CHINO WITH HOMEBOY "SAPO" AT BOYS REPUBLIC.

"I fell into a depression after my marriage ended ... for years," he said. "I felt so rejected."

Within months of that happening, he decided to apply to attend a local air conditioning trade school. He soon earned his certificate and began working the trade. In 1985, he met Maria at a bar. What was considered hooking up as a rebound one night, resulted in an on-and-off-again 13-year relationship, and Mike's second marriage.

Maria already had three children when she and Mike moved in together. Mike grew very close to her kids and acted as their father. He started working more and taking more responsibility. In 1996, he bought his home in Covina—complete with three bedrooms and a pool for the summertime.

Mike and Maria still enjoyed drugs and partying, but somehow they were able to balance this with their working and family lifestyle. Soon, they had Matt together.

In 1998, however, tragedy struck. His stepson, Anthony, was killed in a car accident that was caused by a drunk driver. Mike always respected Anthony because he was such a strong and well-behaved kid. He played football, had good grades, and never caused the family grief. He died at 16.

"When I saw his life taken away, something clicked in my brain," he said. "His death was the beginning of change for me."

Like any mother, Maria took her son's death hard. She started using harder drugs and partying more. Mike was working toward cleaning up his life. That combination resulted in the two separating. He was concerned though because she had custody of their son. He decided to work harder to try and get full-custody on his own, which he ended up doing successfully. After their divorce, he had full-custody of Matt and was able to keep the house.

By this time, he had been working in the air conditioning trade for a while, and had landed a job working at Jet Propulsion Laboratory (JPL) in Pasadena. While he was working to rebuild his personal life, his professional life took a turn for the best.

"There were times when I'd be working in that big building with millions of dollars in equipment around me and think, 'Am I dreaming?'" he remembered. "I wanted to pinch myself. Coming from having nothing, to losing my family, and there I was working at JPL."

IN 2001 THINGS AGAIN CHANGED FOR MIKE. On his way to the JPL's roof, a door hinge came unfastened and the 100-pound-door slammed against his neck as he was walking through it. This resulted in him being rushed to the hospital where they examined him. There they found two things: the door had damaged two disks in his neck; and he had marijuana in his bloodstream.

He was still using drugs here and there when he could. As

a result, he was immediately fired from JPL. Not able to work anywhere else because of his injury, Mike filed a lawsuit with JPL, which lasted five years.

In that time, he depended on his friends to help him keep his house. He stopped using drugs. He tried to focus his attention on his son. By the time the case had settled, he had already started taking classes to earn his credential to teach the air conditioning trade to students. He knew this was his second chance at life, and he was eager to start living it.

"I was 45-years-old when I went to earn my *pinche* vocational credential," he said, laughing. "It took me two years to get. I enjoyed that time. I was excited for something again in my life."

In 2007, Mike earned his vocational credential to teach the air conditioning trade. He earned it by attending satellite campuses for California State University, San Diego, and California State University, Long Beach. By then, he had more than 20 years experience working in the air conditioning trade. He was ready to apply for his first job.

He applied to work with La Puente Regional Occupational Program (ROP) and was given a position at Los Altos High School in Hacienda Heights. It took the school district nearly two years to conduct background checks on him to clear him to work. Despite the numerous times he had been arrested in his lifetime, he had never faced one felony conviction. Once he was cleared, they offered him a full-time position.

"I was so thankful for my job," he said. "When I took it, I didn't think I would be a good role model. But then, I realized, in order to work with kids, you have to be a role model."

As a teacher at a school that is more than 70 percent Latino, Mike said he saw his own reflection in many of his students and in the issues they were facing. They sought advice from him on unhealthy home environments, fitting in, making decisions, and he considered their trust a privilege.

CHINO (RIGHT) AS A TEACHER AT A SAN GABRIEL VALLEY HIGH SCHOOL.

"I did more than just teach in my classroom," he said. "I knew my students on a personal level. I know it's bad to get emotionally attached, but some of those kids just needed someone to talk to them, who understood what they had been through.

"I would hear things from my students that I related to, and I always was able to tell them a piece of my story," he said. "I would try to be the person who said, 'Look, I was there and I went this path.' I wanted them to go the other way; I wanted my students to take the path I didn't.

"See, I learned through trial and error, I look back and think if I had someone to talk to me, who knew what I was going to go through, I think I would have had less heartache in my life."

When reflecting on the habits of today's youth, Mike says that he saw too many of his students lack initiative and only want to work when instant results were promised.

"It's like they depended on too many things, the Internet,

their cell phones, their iPads," he said. "They only cared about things. They didn't want to work for anything because everything they wanted came so easily to them."

Mike also worked with his students' parents to remind them to be involved with their kids and help shape their habits, their likes and dislikes. He encouraged them to pay attention to their kids despite busy work schedules or family duties.

"For me, I look back on why I was the way I was," he said, "and I know it had a lot to do with how I was raised. I just did not get the love or attention I needed. It made me act out at home. Then at school I had no idea what I was doing and had no support at home to help, so I acted out.

"SOME OF THE HARDEST CRIMINALS IN THE WORLD still need something—some type of human connection—and many find it like I did, in gangs. When I see my two boys now, I am always affectionate with them. I talk to them. Even though they hate it, I kiss them and hug them. I am not too hard to show them my love. I know that tomorrow is not a guarantee. I learned to give them what I lacked. I never want them to feel unloved by their dad like I did with mine.

"The only person I had in my life to help me through the good and bad times was my friend, Albert, who I met in the army. He became like a mother/father/mentor to me, but at the same time, he was going through a lot of the same things I was, so instead of lifting each other up, we mostly supported each other side-by-side. He was like my soul mate, but he died of cancer, and even though I have family who are still here, I don't have anyone like him to go to now. He showed me what a true friend really is. Parents need to be there for their kids, it's critical... so critical.

"You see, I believe in timing. There is a reason behind everything that has happened to me and for everything that I have done," he said. "I've been told, 'I'm the only guy that falls into shit and comes out smelling like a rose,' and maybe that's true. The only thing I know is that I'm happy to have come out clean on the other side, where I'm able to now use my life to make a positive difference in the lives of others."

Mike is now pursuing an acting career and rides in real life with biker homie actors Emilio Rivera and Paul Renteria. Mike still resides in Covina, where he is currently enjoying his family. His older son, Mikey, just gave him his first granddaughter, and Matt is in the U.S. Navy.

COYOTE

Freddy "Coyote" Negrete

FREDDY NEGRETE'S FEET FELT HEAVY. The walk to the Intensive Care Unit was not far, but each step felt a mile long. When he opened the door and entered the room, the sound of machines—beeping and pumping air—greeted him. As he looked closer, he realized those machines were keeping his 15-year-old son alive.

Beep.

Beep.

Beep.

Just an hour before, he had received a call that his youngest son, Lorenzo, had been shot. He had hoped that he had been hit in the leg or arm, but his instinct knew better. He had dreamed this before, losing his son. There was no turning back from this moment: the machines or his son's lifeless body.

And just like that, Lorenzo "Frosty" Negrete was gone. Shot in the head and killed due to the same gang violence, on the same streets his father had lived *la vida loca* decades before. Freddy was no stranger to pain and his life had been one filled with struggle, but nothing compared to this.

"I blame myself, even to this day," he said. "I wanted him to stay home, off the streets, but my words fell on deaf ears. From his perspective of my past, I was no moral authority. I was a role model to him, but in the wrong way."

In the ICU room, an energy filled the air, circulating above that hospital bed like a storm gathering. The Negrete family was no stranger to gang violence. Freddy knew that life, but this history went further than him—back to the late 1950s—when Freddy's parents also lived a violent lifestyle as gang members.

Freddy became a ward of the state at the age of 2. A toddler, he and his sister Vicky were put into a foster home after his parents were sent to prison. His mother, a Jewish immigrant, fell hard for his father, a Chicano *pachuco* with gang ties. Their courtship was brief, and soon after having their children, Freddy's father, Fernando, committed armed robbery and was sent to prison. His mother Jacqueline, who had dyed her hair black and joined the Hoyo Maravilla gang, was also sent to prison, but for manslaughter after using a homemade zip gun and shooting another girl in the heart during a fight.

"I remember my sister and I getting out of the car at the foster home and standing on their front lawn and five kids coming out and they were so excited we were there," he said. "They were yelling, 'They're here! They're here!'"

His foster parents were Mormon and white. A baby, really, Freddy grew up using the foster family's last name, Barker. From the outside community, his foster parents were praised for taking in two orphan siblings. They were even named "Foster Parents of the Year" and featured in the *Los Angeles Times*.

APPEARANCES, HOWEVER, ARE NOT ALWAYS what they seem. Behind closed doors, the Barker household was filled with emotional and physical abuse, mostly aimed at Freddy and his sister. In little time, the foster parents' racial prejudice against Chicanos surfaced and they would belittle the children at any opportunity. Their methods of discipline were always physical and Freddy described them as "trying to beat the Mexican out of me."

His older sister had it worse. Her foster father sexually abused her. To scare silence into the children, the foster parents threatened to separate the siblings by sending them to different orphanages.

As a result of this abusive lifestyle, Freddy started to run away from home. He spent a lot of time at Venice Beach, where his light complexion and white surname served as a combination for his first identity—a white surfer kid on the boardwalk.

Without any supervision, at the age of 11 he dropped his first high dosage acid tab. He would leave home for days at a time, sleeping under the pier with close to 40 other runaways. After getting caught, he was taken to the Los Angeles County Juvenile Hall, where he waited for his foster parents to get him. While in a holding cell, Freddy felt nervous. He had grown up in white communities and the blacks and cholos there intimidated him.

Soon after, an older Chicano teenager walked into the cell. His gang name was Buckwheat and he was a member of the Lopez Maravilla gang of East Los Angeles. He was covered in prison-style tattoos. Freddy had never seen anything like that before.

"Maybe because we were the only ones in that holding cell and I was a little surfer kid, Buckwheat was nice to me," he said. "He told me about tattooing, what I needed to make them and how."

When Freddy returned to his foster family's house, he went to his room with a needle and thread and his sister's mascara and started hand poking his first tattoo.

"I was trying to do my name," he remembered, looking down at the faded ink on his hand. "I realized it was a harder process than I had thought. I made it crooked. I was 12-years-old."

During this time, Freddy decided to change his identity. He no longer wanted to be the surfer kid. He spent more time away from home and started getting into more trouble. "I looked for it," he said. "We would break into cars or we would throw rocks through business windows. We were always drinking."

Labeled "incorrigible" by a judge, Freddy was sent to a boys' home, where he met Ruben Martinez, who was a Lomas gang member. Freddy wanted to look and act like Ruben, impressed by his *cholo* style. But Freddy only had what he described as "surfer" clothes that his foster mother had picked out for him. Ruben told Freddy the boys home would take the kids to get clothes and showed him what he needed to have the *cholo* style.

Raised white, Freddy found he had a lot more to learn besides what clothes to wear if he wanted to be a *cholo*. "Ruben

started teaching me how to talk, the slang to use. He even taught me how to stand right."

After his time with Ruben, Freddy wanted to return to San Gabriel. He ran away from the home, not the same young man.

"I went into the barrio," he said. "I found some kids I went to school with and they said, 'Hey, it's Freddy Barker.' I stood tall and said, 'That's not my name. Don't ever call me that. My dad is Mexican. My name is Freddy Negrete. I want to join the barrio.'"

At 13, Freddy was jumped into the Sangra gang and given the gang name Coyote. It was 1969.

"I felt like I found myself finally and found my place with my people," he said. "They took care of each other. That same day, I had a warrant out for my arrest for leaving the boys home and one of my homeboy's families took me in—no questions asked.

"It was almost like I was making my own family with my own friends," he said. As he did this, he learned more about the Latino culture. "I was like a homeless kid then because my foster parents did not want me anymore. The Latino parents let me stay in their homes since I was in the fourth grade. I learned what they eat, all the customs. I learned it all because it was so important to me."

Other kids in the neighborhood only saw him as the white kid trying to be Mexican. This angered Freddy because he wanted to forget that part of him. "Just kids asking if I was Freddy Barker would set me off," he said. "I would fight them right then and there. I realized I had to be tougher to prove myself more."

The neighborhood gave him a sense of loyalty—of family—that Freddy had not had before. "It's the Latino culture thing, I think," he said. "*Cholos* identify with their neighborhood and their loved ones with pride. That's how I wanted to be, that's how I am."

DURING THIS TIME, Freddy was caught and arrested for leaving the boys home and was sent to a juvenile fire camp program. He had a heart murmur so he received a medical hold from the physical aspects of the program and spent the next four months inside the facility. There, he met PomPom, a Maravilla gang member, who also was on medical hold for having his leg amputated. His sister had thrown a record at his leg, cutting it, and the infection resulted in gangrene. PomPom was a great artist. Freddy also had the gift, and the two would spend a lot of time drawing.

"The staff gave us paper because it really kept us busy," he said. "Meeting PomPom was a turning point in my life because he was from Mexico and he knew how to draw the Mexican culture tattoos. He would draw the crosses, ribbons, roses, the *cholos*, and women. I had been tattooing for a couple years by then, so I didn't need to know about the techniques anymore. PomPom taught me the imagery of *cholo* life and culture."

When Freddy returned home, he soon was known as the neighborhood tattoo artist. By age 15, his arms were covered with tattoos.

After the fire camp, Freddy's foster parents agreed to let him live with them again. He also decided he should try and get back into school. At this time, Sangra was engaged in heavy conflict with its rival gang, Lomas. The school counselor did not believe Freddy was ready to return to regular high school. He was placed in a continuation school, where they sent Lomas gang members in the morning and Sangra members in the afternoon. Freddy told the counselor he was not a gang member. The counselor insisted that he was. With Freddy not budging and to make his point, the counselor enrolled Freddy in the morning session with the Lomas members.

Conflict was rising, but was not in full force between the gangs, so things were not as bad as Freddy thought they would be. The kid who taught him how to be a *cholo*, Ruben Martinez, was there. He told other Lomas members that Freddy was cool.

"In class, we would all joke around together, but once we broke for lunch, I had to stay by myself," Freddy recalled.

GRAFFITI WAS A MAIN COMMUNICATOR between the gangs and it sparked tension between them. Freddy remembers when Lomas gang members tagged freeway signs as theirs in neutral territory. To retaliate, Freddy and other Sangra members went to tag over them and crossed them out. At one point, one of Freddy's homeboys went into Lomas and started to cross out other signs there and then signed it "Alex, Tony, Freddy" and their nicknames. On the bus to school, Freddy saw the signs and knew there would be trouble.

"I went to the bathroom and they were all there. I told them I didn't want trouble with them, that I had nothing to do with it, but things were never the same. Chuy was the leader of Lomas then, and we were cool until that day. We became enemies that day to the point that I was in the car when we tried to shoot him."

The days of fistfights and stabbings were few. This was a new era—the time for drive-by shootings. The element of surprise was the weapon of choice, and Freddy remembered seeing many homeboys die. Still, he never feared what was on the other side of guns. He welcomed it, in fact.

"I never killed anybody," he said. "But I remember when I shot someone, wanting to go back to finish him off. It was all or nothing back then."

Jax, a Lomas gang member, was the one he shot. It happened after Jax heard that Freddy was fooling around with the same girl he was with and came out firing six shots at him. To retaliate, Freddy went to Jax's house, knocked on his window and pretended to be a friend of his.

"Hey Jax, it's the homies. It is party time!" Freddy said as he tapped the window. Jax opened it and Freddy shot him. He thought he had killed him until he heard Jax yell out, "You *puto!*" Ready to go back, Freddy's homeboys tried to persuade him to leave. They knew the cops were coming. Frustrated, Freddy complied, but quickly thought of another Lomas enemy of his. They jumped in the car and raced to the guy's house. When they were there, Freddy shot out all of the house's front windows.

By then, it was time to get out of San Gabriel. Racing to the freeway, their car was stopped for speeding. As the cop was about to let them go, a message went out on the radio: "Shooting, two gang members ..." The car was searched, the gun was found, and Freddy was arrested.

HE DIDN'T GO TO STATE PRISON. Instead, a judge sent him to the Preston School of Industry (PSI) and sentenced him to one year. Freddy was not looking for trouble, especially after getting jumped for shooting Lomas members after he was arrested and in L.A. County Jail. But here at PSI, Freddy had an advantage—his artistic talent.

And that talent was sought. Inmates wanted tattoos, portraits, or cards to send home. The staff liked his work and provided him with a job at the print shop. Shortly after he arrived,

Freddy designed the infamous "Smile Now, Cry Later" tattoo after seeing an advertisement for a theatre production. He created fliers that were released to the outside public, which later caught the attention of his future mentor, American tattoo artist Ed Hardy.

With less than 30 days left in his 12-month sentence, Freddy was busted for drug trafficking. He was sentenced to three years in a lock-up facility called the Tamarack Program, which was known for housing violent offenders.

"This place was like an annex, a big castle—it was haunted and had two sides to it. One was the lock-up side for discipline and the other was the program for hard-core youth authority offenders. I had already been sending weed to the inmates there and tattoo patterns when I was on the other side, so they were welcoming to me when I arrived," he said.

"These guys were covered in tattoos. The staff actually supplied them with ink for their tattoo machines," he said. Freddy knew he would be expected to tattoo, but he had guidelines.

"I had policies if anybody tried to pressure me to tattoo them. I wasn't going to tolerate that. I had machines and I would tattoo every day. I was in high demand. My one rule was that I made my own schedule. There would be no line breaking and no exclusivity.

"But guys started cliquing and when you make a clique, you never have a problem with just one guy anymore, but instead with a whole group of guys," he said. "They told me they wanted me to be in their clique and to do all of their tattoos exclusively. I told them they were full of shit."

A fight resulted. Soon after, Freddy became a marked man and he knew he was going to get jumped. The guys at Tamarack, though, were not interested in fighting with fists; nearly all these guys had shanks. Instead of giving in to the demands of the clique to turn on one of his homeboys, Freddy faced the chance of getting stabbed to death.

The next day, Freddy was confronted in the kitchen and stabbed multiple times and kicked unconscious. He woke up in

the hospital not knowing who or where he was. Everyone assumed he would go back under "protective custody," to avoid further conflict. Not Freddy—he insisted on going back. His reputation was on the line. Surprising the clique that nearly killed him when he returned, they decided he had heart and left him alone.

Freddy continued tattooing, impressing the staff with his talent. Soon the staff approved an early release date for him.

On the outside, Chicanos were requesting colorless tattoos, but most shops were offering the "Sailor Jerry" looking, more traditional tattoos. There was nothing "fine lined," or with the Black & Gray look that Chicanos pioneered and is so popular today. Jack Rudy, an artist at Good Time Charlie's tattoo studio (who also is known as a master in Black & Gray tattooing), had seen Freddy's work and wanted to meet him.

Jack had created an extended needle that could tattoo a finer line, making a tattoo smoother and more photo-like. Using that needle, Freddy's artistic talent impressed Jack after he tattooed a fish on Jack's leg. Good Time Charlie's had just been bought by Ed Hardy—world-renowned tattoo pioneer and owner of the multimillion dollar clothing company empire that holds his name. Ed saw something special that Freddy could bring to his shop. Freddy knew Chicano culture and he learned the art from growing up in the barrio and through his prison time—he offered something authentic and different. He was hired.

After two years of Ed Hardy's mentorship, Freddy's tattooing was at an entirely different level and people were beginning to notice. In 1980, he was named "Tattoo Artist of the Year" at

the Fifth World Tattoo Convention.

A few years later, Freddy married Patricia and had his first son, Isaiah. He was 23 and remembered feeling how he felt ready for fatherhood. "All my friends already had kids," he said. "I had my tattooing job. We had our house. I was really ready."

DURING THIS TIME, Freddy also struggled with heroin addiction and had an affiliation for "super cools" (cigarettes dipped in PCP). His dependency and extramarital affairs led him to a point where he was ready to change his ways. He soon joined Victory Outreach, an evangelical organization aimed at reforming homeboys from gang life violence or substance abuse.

He made the decision to give his life to Christ. He stopped drugs. He stopped tattooing.

"I was told that tattooing was the work of the devil," he said. "So I quit at Good Time Charlie's. I remember telling Jack Rudy, 'I'm serving the Lord now.'"

This religious awakening led Freddy to later join a church

called The Brethrens of Christ. He spent time in Amish country and came back ordained.

He started serving as pastor at his own church, The Living Word Brethren in Christ, dressing in custom-made Zoot Suits and inspiring his congregation with his powerful testimonies. He was a man of God and this transformation brought Patricia and their marriage back into his life.

Shortly after, he was caught cheating on her and the relationship ended. Ashamed of his actions, Freddy left his role as a pastor and started using again. A few years later, he had a job, but still struggled with drug addiction. To feed his habit, he started burglarizing homes. Sometimes, he would do it on his lunch breaks.

During this time, he met his second wife, Anabeth, who soon became pregnant with Lorenzo. News of her pregnancy made Freddy want to change his ways, so he went on a Methadone program to get straight. They made plans to move to Palm Springs to have a fresh start.

The Los Angeles Police Department had other plans. They had found Freddy's prints inside a home and he was up on a burglary charge. With the help of a lawyer, he made bail and was not sentenced for two years. During that time, he was clean and was taking his fatherhood role seriously. The cops testified he had changed. His sentence was reduced from three years to one. In 1989, he returned to the Los Angeles County Jail.

Freddy's talent impressed the staff there so much that the jail captain asked him to paint a large Los Angeles Sheriff's Department (LASD) badge as a backdrop for press conferences. For his services, he was allowed to eat in the Officers Dining Room. Freddy's talent then caught the attention of Sheriff Sherman Block, who went on to become the highest paid elected official in the country during his tenure. Mr. Block wanted a badge designed by Freddy for his dining room wall.

In time, Freddy created a design that was officially approved and used for a fleet of LASD's police cars. He met Mr. Block once and while they did not speak to each other, Mr.

Block instructed the wardens to give Freddy access to his personal refrigerator, resulting in Freddy's meals consisting of prime ribs, steaks, and more. Soon after, he was released on three years' probation.

Once he was out, some time went by and Freddy felt restless with his life situation. He thought back to when he was tattooing and wondered if the best times of his life were behind him.

He hadn't touched a tattoo gun in 10 years.

He called Jack Rudy.

Jack told Freddy that he was welcome back to the tattooing scene. Not only had he been missed, but his work had become legendary. Black & Gray was sought after in the tattoo world and the work that Freddy knew how to do was the work that people wanted.

The first gig Jack had for Freddy was in San Diego. When Freddy picked up that tattoo gun, he felt the adrenaline pump in his veins. Indeed, he was back.

FREDDY WAS NOW KNOWN as the founder of Black & Gray tattoos. His expertise was even sought after by Oscar-winning Director Taylor Hackford, while he was working on the 1993 film "Blood In, Blood Out," which involved three relatives who are in a gang and how this impacts their lives. The director needed the tattoos to look authentic, and it was Freddy who made the tattoos look real. More than 30 movie productions sought Freddy's perspective and expertise, and over the years, he worked with big-time Hollywood directors, including James Cameron and William Friedkin.

Even with this success, Freddy could not free himself from his drug addiction. To avoid a drug test, he skipped a visit with his probation officer and put himself in violation of his parole. His ex-wife Patricia had Isaiah, and Lorenzo was with his wife Anabeth. Freddy decided to turn himself in—he knew he had about a year to serve if he did. That would give him time to get clean. Then, he could work to meet his latest goal—to open his

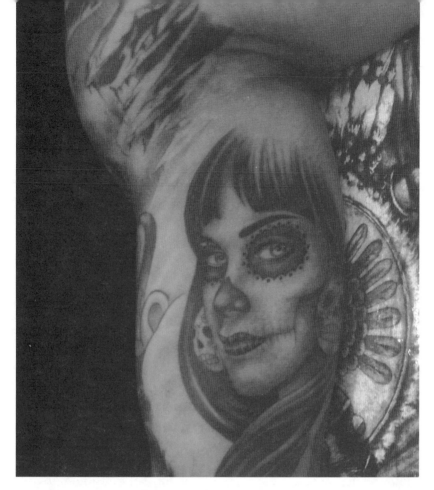

own tattoo shop in Santa Barbara.

Freddy left Hollywood behind to turn himself in, and he soon found himself behind bars. His artistic talent proved helpful there again. He returned to drawing murals and in return for his services, he was given an "emergency overcrowding release." There was no emergency, but his talent had freed him again.

Soon after his release, Freddy's shop, Ratatattoo, opened in Santa Barbara. It had a 1930s theme and his clientele ranged from bikers and musicians to construction workers to cops and sheriffs. The shop was a success and soon Freddy moved Anabeth and Lorenzo to Santa Barbara to be with him, while also working on movie productions again. Everything was finally falling into place.

Or so it seemed, until the demons of addiction returned. In little time, his marriage, his family and his business started to spiral out of Freddy's control. Then, his shop was accused of tattooing a minor. Her parents sued and the shop eventually closed as a result.

"It wasn't just the end of my business," he said. "It was the end of my American Dream."

Anabeth soon left him and took Lorenzo with her. Freddy thought it would be a good time to take his older son to Hawaii to try and make ends meet there. By then, Isaiah had been tattooing for years. Despite their talent, they struggled and only stayed in Hawaii for a few months. Freddy's longtime friend Gill Montie had his shop, Tattoo Mania in West Hollywood. When Gill reached out and offered Freddy and his son a regular gig at his shop, things felt as if they were finally going to improve.

WORK BECAME STEADY and Freddy hustled to tattoo and work on movie productions, but he still was partying hard. He loved his sons, but he was not living by example. At this time, Anabeth reached out to Freddy about Lorenzo, who was having major issues in school. She could not control him and she told Freddy she was ready to send him to a juvenile institution to help set him straight.

"I knew she was desperate," Freddy said. "But, I had grown up in institutions, bouncing from foster home to juvenile centers and then to the California Youth Authority. I also knew where those places took me—the streets, to gang banging, and eventually to prison. That was not the fate of my son. I fought for custody and won. Lorenzo would be with me."

Freddy had not realized how deep into *la vida loca* Lorenzo was. He would disappear for days at a time. Soon, Freddy learned that Lorenzo had become a Sangra gang member and was gang-banging hard. Then, one night, Lorenzo came home with a gun.

"I was devastated," Freddy said. "I was consumed with fear

for my 15-year-old son. I felt as if I was watching the hand of destiny. I knew something was coming and it was going to be awful.

"But who was I to tell him what to do or not do? Not even 30 years before him, I was out and doing the exact same thing," he said. "Like I said, I was a role model, but the wrong kind."

Lorenzo's gang name was Frosty. Ironically, it was the same nickname Lorenzo had as a baby. "He looked like a little snowman so we called him that," Freddy remembered. Now "RIP Frosty" rests forever in an inked tribute around the front of Freddy's neck. "My little baby boy... I lost him."

Freddy never found out exactly what happened the night that Lorenzo was shot. It appears that someone walked up to him and shot him. Shootings became the main method of madness and retaliation since Freddy's own gang days, which included guns, but more often involved fistfights or stabbings. Decades later, during Lorenzo's time, the goal was to not miss your target. Drive-bys and walk-bys were best for this.

Freddy does not yearn for revenge for his son's death since he blames himself so much. In the months after Lorenzo's death, Freddy found it hard to get up in the morning and returned to drugs to numb himself enough to function. Soon he was arrested and sent to prison. While Freddy was there, the one who suffered the most was his older son, Isaiah. He was devastated at the death of his brother and he was alone, living in someone's garage, tattooing. Freddy worked to get clean while in prison, but the years of drug use had major consequences to his health. He suffered from congestive heart failure. Nevertheless, upon his release, he found Isaiah and the two returned to Hollywood to tattoo and live together.

Freddy's heart problems grew worse. At one point, the doctors told him the only solution would be a heart transplant. They told him that his heart was enlarged and that he was dying. He was still using and was caught and sent to the Los Angeles County Jail again, but this time he could no longer walk, confined to a wheelchair, and weak. He suffered from

three heart attacks there. He called his son and told him not to visit him. He did not want Isaiah to see him that way.

"I still had my Christian background, you know," he said. "And I decided I needed to really talk to God. I remember in order to find a place to be alone, I had to go up these two flights of stairs. It took me more than 45 minutes because at each step I had to regain my strength. When I made it up there, I prayed and told God I could not make any promises and that I was not asking for Him to do anything in return for what I would do because I knew that I had failed Him before. Instead I remembered a passage in the Old Testament, wherein the prophet came to him and told him he was going to die and he went directly to God and asked for more time and God gave him 16 years. So I quoted that passage and asked for more time. I did not want to die that way. My son needed me. Please God, don't let me die in jail."

The next morning, Freddy had another heart attack. On the way to the hospital, Freddy felt different—this time, he felt the touch of God. Two weeks later, doctors reported improvement. His heart was functioning better than before. He was able to eat again and was sleeping better. In little time, he did not need the wheelchair. Doctors were perplexed—Freddy's recovery was nothing short of a miracle.

"I knew I would never use again after that," said Freddy, who has remained clean since 2007. His recovery was supported by the Beit T'Shuvah ("Returning Home"), a treatment facility based on Jewish spirituality and Twelve Step principles. He spent six months there, where he made peace with God, himself, and with Lorenzo's death.

Currently, Freddy tattoos at the Shamrock Social Club in West Hollywood with his son Isaiah. The two live together. He also volunteers his time with Beit T'Shuvah, helping young heroin addicts recover from the same struggles he endured.

A book about his life, *Smile Now, Cry Later: Guns, Gangs, and Tattoos—My Life in Black and Gray,* by Freddy Negrete with Steve Jones, was released in 2016 by Seven Stories Press, New York City.

CHUY

Jesse "Chuy" Olivas

JESSE OLIVAS WAS HAVING A BAD LOW from the drugs he had consumed earlier in the evening. Just a few hours prior, he was planning how to get arrested again. Prison was where he belonged. Everything made sense to him in prison. He knew how to act, how to be... there were simply too many feelings, too much responsibility on the outside.

I'll rob a liquor store, he remembered thinking. Maybe I can break into a house and just wait for the police to come. Anything for the familiarity that incarceration brought to him. Everything would have worked out if his ex, Dora, didn't contact him to come over and stay.

He lay on the couch wondering what he was doing there in their old apartment. He looked around the place and knew it was no longer home. He closed his eyes and let his mind wander back toward his plan.

The room was dark and out of the stillness he heard someone shuffling. He did not bother to open his eyes; he was not in the mood for another lecture from his ex. The steps grew closer. He pretended to be asleep.

It was then he felt a tiny hand touch his forearm. It was his 4-year-old daughter, Jessica. Her little hand felt clammy, almost as if she were nervous to wake him. Her round face, dark hair and kiddie pajamas made Chuy sit upward to face her. In the darkness and with the little light shining in from the alley street lamp outside, he thought his daughter looked like an angel.

"Daddy," she whispered. "Are you OK?"

Chuy took a moment to imagine how he looked. He was still sweating from the aftermath of the drugs and he knew he probably looked tired from not sleeping. He did not want to alarm her.

"Oh baby," he said. "Daddy is fine. I just don't feel too good right now, that's all."

She leaned in closer to him. He could feel the warmth of her breath, her weight against his shoulder. Her wide eyes stared straight into his and it felt as if they reached his very core.

Without any hesitation, she whispered to him, "Don't worry, Daddy. I will be here for you. I'll always be here to take care of you. I love you, don't worry."

Chuy stared at her and she repeated herself, as if she knew he needed to hear her words again. "I'll be here Daddy," and with that she wrapped her little arms around him to reassure him how serious she was.

Chuy's eyes began to water. His entire life, he felt something was missing, and there she was offering nothing but unconditional love. The kind that does not stop loving when you break the law or disappoint someone, that was the kind of love he craved. He sought it out numerous times from women, but they would grow tired of his ways and either break it off or send him on his way, off and running.

And now, in the early twilight of the morning, the smallest and youngest person Chuy knew was offering him what he had been searching for all his life. He knew that he had not been an ideal father to little Jessica, but he also knew that none of his past mattered to her. She loved him just because that's what she knew how to do.

He held onto his daughter's words the whole night, long after she fell asleep on the couch with him. Suddenly, he realized how close to turning 40 he was. It was time to become a better father, a better man, or at the very least, someone better.

When the sun rose the next morning, Chuy knew he would never be the same again. As the light broke through the dark-

CHUY WITH HIS BROTHER.

ness and a new day began, he decided to use that morning to start living his life.

Getting to that morning, however, was not easy for Chuy. Growing up in the projects of Aliso Village in Boyle Heights, he hardly had a relationship with his biological parents. He was given to his father's sister Lydia when he was a baby, and she raised him as her own with her husband Ventura and their children. He called his aunt "mom" from the start.

As a child, Chuy saw his father every so often and never met his mother. Deep inside, he wondered why they did not have more interest in him. His thoughts soon turned to resentment and when he was in grade school, it took little for him to lose his temper and act out what he was feeling.

In 1967, the family moved to South San Gabriel. Going to school there was more challenging for Chuy as many of his new classmates did not welcome him. This posed a problem for him from his first day.

"I remember the white kids saying, 'We'll get that wetback after school,'" he said. "I never thought of us as Mexican-American or different. There was no prejudice in my house. Being treated that way was not how I was raised. I could not help but fight it."

Around the age of 11, Chuy found himself getting into more and more trouble in school. He was getting suspended and found himself drawn to trouble instead of trying to avoid it.

"I had a lot of insecurities as a kid that started with me not having my own parents raising me... I never felt good enough," he said. "Then I felt isolated at school from the racism. I decided to hang out with the older guys. I felt as if I could identify more with them."

LIVING IN HIS AUNT'S HOUSE, he considered all of her children his cousins. They often played together in the house. One day, Lydia told Chuy that his older cousin Mitchell was actually his older brother. It had turned out that their mother had given him to Lydia to raise as well.

Instead of this news bringing Chuy closer to his sibling, he felt a distance form between him and his brother. For years, Mitchell had been a top student, involved in school—Chuy never felt they had anything in common. For years he only saw him as his cousin, not his older brother. The news only made him feel different and isolated from someone he shared blood with—how could they be brothers if they were so unalike?

Soon afterward, Chuy joined the neighborhood gang. As a member of Las Lomas, S.S.G, he found himself hanging out regularly with older guys. One night, all of them were shooting up heroin and Chuy wanted to try it. He was 14-years-old.

"I still remember those guys. I hung out with them because I felt as if they were looking out for me," he said. "I wanted to try the drug. A few of the guys went back and forth with the idea because they knew I was young. Man, I still remember

that first hit though—I tried it and I was hooked."

Over the next year Chuy was in juvenile hall for burglary and possession of heroin. After serving his sentence, he went back to high school. Still struggling with his identity, Chuy was known as a gang member by his peers, but still managed to participate in regular school activities. One year, he danced Mexican *folklórico* in a school competition they won. He only participated in the event because he had a "thing" for one of the girl dancers, even though he admitted winning the competition made him feel good inside.

"I never was a bad kid," he said. "I came from a good home where everyone sat around the table to eat dinner. I just did not know how to be one thing or how to be balanced. I did not aspire or want to only be a gang member, but I also did not know how to only be something else either."

The summer after graduation, Chuy decided to take a girl out on a date. Later that evening, they necked in the back of his Volkswagen Bug. Suddenly he heard commotion out on the street and he went to go see what was happening.

A fight was in progress. One guy was beating another guy with a shovel. Trying to help the guy getting beaten, Chuy reached for the shovel and removed it from the other guy's reach. Within minutes, the police arrived, and when they did, they saw Chuy with the shovel in his hands. He ran. He looked guilty enough and his past record did not give the police much reason to want to investigate.

A few weeks later, Chuy wanted to go out with some friends to get high. The group of guys he was meeting up with had robbed a liquor store earlier that night. Chuy left the house with anticipation and the police were waiting down the street for them. All of them were arrested. When the storeowner identified the robbers, he immediately pointed to Chuy as one of those who held a gun, even though he was not involved.

He was arrested and had two charges against him: assault with a deadly weapon and robbery. In court, he was sentenced to serve an indeterminate sentence and was sent to the Youth Authority Center in Ontario.

By his 21st birthday, Chuy was still in the facility and did not know when he was going to be released. The "indeterminate sentence" he was given meant he would be free when the facility freed him.

If he had been over the age of 21 when the incidents occurred, he would have been sentenced to serve about six months in county jail for the misdemeanor offenses. Instead, he had no idea when he would go free. The Youth Authority's board determined his fate—whether he was able to remain incarcerated or go home.

Chuy's lawyers appealed how the sentencing came down, questioning whether a misdemeanor offense committed between the ages of 16 and 21 could constitutionally hold up since at Youth Authority, Chuy could serve a term longer than the maximum jail term for someone over the age of 21.

After being in various courthouses, Chuy's case eventually made it to the United States Supreme Court. On June 22, 1976, in The People v. Jesús Macias Olivas, the Supreme Court decided it was unconstitutional to hold youth in Youth Authority for any period of time that was longer than the maximum jail term that might be imposed for a person more than 21-years-of-age.

Two days before his 21st birthday, the Court made its decision. Chuy remembers how a priest who worked at the Center pulled him aside and asked him if his full name was Jesús Macias Olivas. When he told the priest that it was, the priest showed him an article in the *LA Times* that said Jesse was set to go free as a result of the court's decision.

And as quickly as the judgment was declared, he was back on the outside. While he was glad to be released, a fury brewed inside of him. He felt the system had cheated him out of years of his life by wrongfully keeping him in the Youth Authority Center.

"I felt as if someone owed me something for the time I lost," he said.

CHUY IN SAN QUENTIN STATE PRISON.

Shortly after his release Chuy met Camille. They dated for a while. Soon Camille told Chuy she was expecting. She wanted him to settle down so they could start a family, but he was too involved with the neighborhood, drinking, and drugs.

In 1978, Chuy was sent to prison for armed robbery. While Camille was getting ready to have his baby girl, he was sent to San Quentin State Prison. He had a five-year sentence.

"Most of the guys I grew up with in juvenile hall and met

in Youth Authority were there with me in prison," he remembered. "I felt like I was home again. The prisons nowadays are different. I felt at home with these guys. It was the same group of us, just in a different place.

"I never felt threatened and nothing bad happened to me in prison. I knew the guys. I had nothing to fear. Back then you could study different trades in there. I was a plumber. I read a lot. I worked out when I could. I adapted really well to the prison life."

Chuy had no problem serving his sentence until Lydia, the woman who raised him, who he loved like a mother, died. He was not allowed to attend her funeral services.

"I knew me being in there was hard for her," he said. "When she died I felt lost. I felt so helpless because I could not go and pay my respects. Whenever I got out of a placement, each time, she was right there waiting for me on the outside—this would be the first time I would get out... alone."

EVEN THOUGH CHUY WAS ALONE when he was released from San Quentin, his solitude was not long lasting. He went to see his daughter, who was now 5-years-old, to meet her for the first time. Camille had moved on from their relationship, but both she and Chuy felt it was important for Cecelia to know her father.

Chuy went back to his old acquaintances and friends. His actions would result in him serving six-to-eight-month sentences in the county jail on different occasions.

One night, he met Nelly and they started dating. Soon after, she told him she was pregnant. They were both using heroin, and Chuy knew when little Jesse Jr. was born that something had to change. He decided to get clean and raise his son on his own.

Before he could do this, he had to serve some time at the county jail. While there, he stayed sober and away from drugs. Before he was released, a new charge was added to his file, but this time it was manslaughter. He chose to plea bargain,

CHUY WITH HIS OLD HOMIES.

pleaded guilty, and more time was added to his sentence. Back to prison he went.

When he was released, he knew Nelly was not waiting for him. He decided to go to a bar in Lincoln Heights. He met Dora there. She was a teacher for a local school district. They hit it off immediately and he went home with her... and decided to stay. Soon, his youngest daughter, Jessica was born. After her birth, Chuy and Dora decided to get married.

Chuy felt a sense of security while he was married to Dora. She took care of everything. She paid the rent and the bills and managed the household. He was working as a truck driver and would simply turn over his checks to her, letting her handle all responsibility.

"I think I felt like she was another mom to me," he said. "She was like the one I had lost and the one I never had."

Despite Dora taking care of him, their marriage only lasted 18 months. He soon felt too dependent on her. He also saw her as controlling over time.

"I started sneaking out to hang out with the guys," he said. "I'd do dumb things just to do them. I did not want to be a person that was being controlled all the time. One night I came home loaded and she told me to leave."

"Ironically, her doing what I knew was coming was the thing I feared the most. Her telling me to leave was like losing my mom all over again. I did not know how to be completely alone. It was the scariest thing for me—to have to figure out how to be by myself."

Upon separating, Chuy felt as if he hit rock bottom. He started initiating fights and using drugs more. He had no idea how to pick up the pieces of his life. She handled his credit cards and bills—he never learned how. Within a short time he lost everything.

"I felt as if us separating was like an affirmation that I did not deserve anything, that I couldn't do anything on my own that was good or right," he said.

He started living on the streets. Within that first year of being separated, he was shot in the neck randomly while at a local 7-11 convenience store and was stabbed three times in three separate gang incidents.

Still using during this time, Chuy realized he wanted to die. One rainy night, he asked God to take his life. He was only 37-years-old. "I felt as if I had nothing to show for my life, and I would never amount to anything," he said. "The next morning, when I woke up, I figured God had a sense of humor keeping me here."

It was around this time, after every foundation he had crumbled down around him, when that moment occurred of his youngest daughter Jessica touching his forehead. As the sun began to shine through the windows of his ex's apartment, Chuy started to plan what he had to do to get his life in order.

He decided to go back to work, driving big rig trucks. He applied to a job in Pomona, and explained before they hired him that he was trying to piece his life together and had some issues, but really needed to work. The vice president of the company asked Chuy if he could talk to him outside. Once there, he asked Chuy if his problem was that he had lost his license. Chuy told him no. The vice president pushed for more information and finally asked Chuy what the problem was.

"I told him I was still on drugs and speed-balling," he said. "I also told him I was not sure how to stop."

BY CHANCE, THE VICE PRESIDENT was a recovering alcoholic and a 12-step member. He told Chuy that he needed to give himself time to heal and recover. He later arranged for Chuy to enter a rehabilitation center in Pasadena, where he spent four months sobering up and learning why changing his life was so critical.

"I knew I was going to live or I was going to die, and both could come at anytime," he said. "I started realizing I did not want to die overdosing on drugs. I also learned I had issues with my family and my older brother in particular. I was envious of the success he had—if we were treated the same growing up, why was I so different than him?

"I had to learn why I thought the way I did—I also needed some direction on what to do with this new life of mine."

Chuy left the facility in September 1993, clean of drugs, and he has remained that way to this day. Whenever he felt challenged by his life or had the feeling of wanting to go back to his old ways, he always thought of the conversation he had with little Jessica that night on the couch after she asked if he was okay. That always inspired him to steer clear of any such temptations.

He left the rehab center and began working full-time. His relationships with his children strengthened and life was making sense. In time, he met Maia, a younger woman, married her, and together they bought the home Chuy still resides in today in Covina, California.

Their marriage did not last long. Maia began to take sleeping pills and grew distant from him. Despite his love for her,

he knew her behavior was not positive for either him or his children. Chuy divorced her. They had been married six years.

By the time the divorce was final, he had full custody of both Jesse Jr., who was 15 at the time, and Jessica, who was 12. The three of them lived in the house together and he enjoyed being a single father. He would make dinner, attend their school activities, and help them with their homework.

"We were finally a family," he said.

While working, Chuy also started to go to various juvenile halls, prisons, and some local schools to share his story and help them understand that there are different paths to take.

"I tell them, you are not obligated to join a gang," he said. "The only limits our kids today have are the ones they put on themselves. We all have the ability, and I really try to emphasize this to them, to step up and rise above everything."

Life was finally how Chuy had always wanted it to be. In 2007, he met his current wife, Raquel. They dated for more than a year, and married on his birthday: June 20, 2008.

"She does a lot for me. I don't have to nag at her. I don't control her. She is my wife and my love for her is based on trust," he said. "We work together and go together in the same direction. There is nothing that we cannot talk about. There is nothing we won't tell each other. I finally feel as if I have found my life partner."

Upon looking at Chuy, it is hard to imagine he was addicted to heroin for more than 20 years. Even he admits it is hard to describe the power the drug had over him during those times in his life.

"I hit rock bottom because of the drug," he said. "I wanted to stop for many years, but simply did not know how. It's not easy to quit. In fact, heroin dictates everything."

"At one point, I knew it controlled me more than it should have. It took me places I never wanted to go or be. It made me want to die. Looking back, I realize that the drug never controlled my destiny. Only I could do that. And once I decided to change my life, I could. For someone to say that they cannot stop using... I will not believe them—they just need to learn how to stop."

Chuy continues to be a speaker for at-risk youth and prison inmates whenever he can. His goal is to share his story with as many people as possible so they can find their paths. He is also still driving trucks and enjoys the solitude a long drive brings him.

He and Raquel live in their home in Covina with her two younger children. His children, Cecelia, Jesse Jr., and Jessica all reside in California. He has three grandsons and two granddaughters.

Alisha M. Rosas was born and raised in the Inland Empire. She is an advocate for educational access and equal rights for all. In 2007, she wrote the first book the United Farm Workers published in two decades, *California's Broken Promises: The Laws on the Books are not the Laws in the Fields.* She is a believer in second chances, hope, and is inspired by the idea that all things will work out in the end. She resides in Ontario, CA with her husband, Carlos, and their two children, Diego and Rosie.

Luis J. Rodriguez wrote one of the most important books about Los Angeles street gangs after the 1992 L.A. Uprising: *Always Running, La Vida Loca, Gang Days in L.A.* In 2001, *Hearts &Hands: Creating Community in Violent Times"* appeared, summarizing thirty years of Luis's work. Another memoir, *It Calls You Back: An Odyssey Through Love, Addiction, Revolutions, and Healing,* came out in 2011. He is founding editor of Tia Chucha Press and co-founder of Tia Chucha's Cultural Center & Bookstore. Luis served as the official Poet Laureate of Los Angeles from 2014-2016.